RUSSIAN FORMALIST CRITICISM

Russian Formalist Criticism
Four Essays
SECOND EDITION

*Translated and
with an introduction by*
Lee T. Lemon
and
Marion J. Reis

New introduction by
Gary Saul Morson

UNIVERSITY OF NEBRASKA PRESS • LINCOLN AND LONDON

© 1965 by the University of Nebraska Press
Introduction by Gary Saul Morson © 2012 by the Board of Regents of the
University of Nebraska
Manufactured in the United States of America

First Nebraska paperback printing: 1965

Library of Congress Cataloging-in-Publication Data
Russian formalist criticism: four essays / translated and with an introduc-
tion by Lee T. Lemon and Marion J. Reis; new introduction by Gary Saul
Morson.—Second edition.
pages; cm
Includes bibliographical references and index.
ISBN 978-0-8032-3998-2 (paperback: alkaline paper)
1. Formalism (Literary analysis) 2. Literature, Modern. I. Lemon, Lee
T. II. Reis, Marion J. III. Morson, Gary Saul, 1948– IV. Shklovskii, Viktor,
1893–1984. Iskusstvo kak priëm. English. V. Shklovskii, Viktor, 1893–1984.
"Tristram Shendi" Sterna i teoriia romana. English. VI. Tomashevskii, B.
V. (Boris Viktorovich), 1890–1957. Tematika. English. VII. Eikhenbaum,
Boris Mikhailovich, 1886–1959. Teoriia "formal'nogo metoda". English.
VIII. Title: Art as technique. IX. Title: Sterne's Tristram Shandy. X. Title:
Thematics. XI. Title: Theory of the "formal method".
PN98.F6R87 2012
801'.950947—dc23   2011050454

Introduction

Gary Saul Morson

A century after the Russian Formalist movement began, and a half
century since the present translation brought it to American readers,
we can appreciate its enormous importance.[1] One could almost say
that literary theory has evolved into a series of footnotes to Formalism.
Further developed by Prague structuralists and later by structuralists in France and around the world, the key concepts of Formalism
have shaped thought across the humanities and social sciences. Even
theorists who explicitly reject Formalism have shown its profound
influence in defining what needs to be rejected. The various schools
we have come to call post-structuralist develop Formalist tenets, directly or by inversion.

The Formalists' intellectually strongest opponents, the circle of
Mikhail Bakhtin, first enunciated their ideas as a respectful if vigorous
critique of Formalist assumptions.[2] Bakhtin used his opposition to
Formalism as a springboard to create a set of counter-theories that
have arguably proven to be the strongest contributions to literary
theory since Aristotle. Neither the Formalists nor Bakhtin can be
properly understood outside their debate with each other.

Russian Science

In ways Americans often do not appreciate, Formalism reflects important trends in Russian thought. Dostoevsky once observed that a
Russian intellectual is someone who can read Darwin and promptly
resolve to become a pickpocket (for the good of the people, of course).
That is, Russians take ideas to their extreme, as if the greater the
violation of common sense, the better. They find it hard to resist the
appeal of "lefter than thou" thinking, and having gone as far as possible, they discover salvational implications in the most unlikely theses.
Dostoevsky had in mind the Russian nihilist's discovery of spiritual
exhilaration in extreme materialism. One radical famously saw in the

"dissected frog" (which somehow demonstrated the nonexistence of the soul) the salvation of the Russian people. Or as Dostoevsky also liked to say, Russians do not just become atheists, they have faith in atheism. They are converted to it, and treat leaders who die in a state of unbelief as martyrs.

Dostoevsky would not have been surprised at the extreme doctrines or tone characteristic of the Russian Formalists. In their passionate coldness, the Formalists belonged to a Western intellectual tradition the Russians took especially seriously: the idea that it is possible to construct a true social *science*, as hard as physics. Elie Halévy has famously called such thinking "moral Newtonianism." As Newton had reduced the dizzying complexity of planetary motion to three laws of motion plus the law of universal gravitation, so his followers aspired to do the same for the human and social worlds. Economics, the psyche, culture, ethics, politics—indeed, everything in human life—could be studied like physics, allowing for iron-clad laws and predictability. Surely to think otherwise must be sheer sentimentality, or still worse, the legacy of religion and superstition! We find this faith in social science in thinkers as diverse as Locke, Condorcet, Laplace, Bentham, Marx, Freud, Malinowski, Lévi-Strauss, B. F. Skinner, Milton Friedman, and Jared Diamond. Before Auguste Comte coined the word "sociology," he intended to name his new discipline "social physics."

It is well known that modern economics has claimed to have achieved the status of a hard science and to have offered mathematical models of all (not just economic) human behavior. As Gary Becker has put the point, "The economic approach provides a valuable unified framework for understanding *all* human behavior. . . . Human behavior can be viewed as involving participants who maximize their utility from a stable set of preferences and accumulate an optimal amount of information and other inputs. . . . [T]he economic approach provides a unified framework for understanding behavior that has long been sought by and eluded Bentham, Comte, Marx and others."[3] It is less well known that modern economic theory was explicitly modeled on Newtonian astronomy (or, rather, what was taken to be Newtonian astronomy). Among Becker's predecessors in formulating the economic approach, Léon Walras, whose last

work was titled *Économique et Mécanique,* formulated the notion of
economic equilibrium as a parallel to the equilibrium (that is, stabil-
ity) of planetary motion.[4]

This kind of thinking proved especially strong in the first land to
adopt "scientific socialism." Russians found particularly seductive the
sort of scientism that claimed not only to explain events but also to
control them for human salvation. The Bolsheviks represented only
one strain of such thought.

LITERARINESS

The Formalists exemplified this approach by turning it on its head.
They, too, claimed to have developed a hard science but inverted
the theories of their putatively scientific predecessors. They rejected
"sociological" reductions of literature to nonliterary forces. The sociologists, especially Marxists, had reasoned that if we know the laws
of economics, and if the laws of economics shape all of culture, and
if literature is just another branch of culture, then we *already* have
a science of literature. Other movements claimed to have different
sociological keys. For the Formalists, all these movements failed the
test of science.

To begin with, the sociologists did not have a *consistent* theory but (in
practice) borrowed incompatible ideas as current polemic dictated.
They were guilty of mere "eclecticism" (a favorite Formalist term of
abuse). Moreover, they were closed to empirical disconfirmation.
Boris Eichenbaum's essay "The Theory of the 'Formal Method'"
takes the form of a history because, he explains, the Formalists are
not dogmatists but scientists, and scientific theories change as they
are tested against facts. When the Formalists found a theory challenged by a set of previously unconsidered facts or by application to
a new topic, they reformulated it. Then they repeated the process
again and again. There is no ready-made "formal method," Eichenbaum concludes, only a scientific approach to literature. This unusual
readiness for disconfirmation remains one of the most unusual and
appealing aspects of Russian Formalism.

Eichenbaum's classic essay (the fourth selection in the present
volume) describes Formalism "not as a dogmatic system but as a
historical summation":

Our scientific approach has had no such prefabricated program or doctrine, and has none. In our studies we value a theory only as a working hypothesis to help us discover and interpret facts. . . . We posit specific principles and adhere to them insofar as the material justifies them. If the material demands their refinement or change, we change or refine them. In this sense we are quite free from our own theories—as science must be free to the extent that theory and conviction are distinct. There is no ready-made science; science lives not by settling on truth, but by overcoming error. (102–3)

Above all, the Formalists rejected the sociologists' attempt to explain literature in terms of extraliterary social forces. Such forays led to absurdities such as explanations of Gogol's humor by his class origin as a small landowner. Literature must be explained in terms taking cognizance of the literary. To explain something one must first understand it, and one cannot even begin to understand literature unless one first understands it *as* literature.

How can one develop a science of some set of phenomena, they asked, when those very phenomena are not even properly seen—when their very integrity is denied? Mathematicians live in society, and their work must somehow reflect history (because everything does), but surely to understand the history of mathematics one must first learn how to solve an equation or grasp a proof! Can one understand physics knowing only the sociology or biography of physicists? If so, why do we still teach physics as a separate discipline?

By the same token, the Formalists contended, before we formulate a science of literature we must understand literature, and that means grasping precisely what is *literary* about it. Eichenbaum cites Roman Jakobson's well-known (and very Russian) methodological statement:

The object of the science of literature is not literature, but literariness—that is, that which makes a given work a work of literature. Until now literary historians have preferred to act like the policeman who, intending to arrest a certain person, would, at any opportunity, seize any and all persons who chanced into the apartment, as well as those who passed along the street. The literary historians used everything—anthropology, psychology, politics, philosophy. Instead of a science of literature, they created a conglomeration of homespun disciplines. (107)

But what exactly is "literariness"? What makes a literary work "literary"? As Jakobson's tone suggests, the Formalists' answers to these questions typically adopted a nihilistic manner. It was as if they tried to outdo the sociological reductionists with a still more shocking Formalist reductionism. Épater les marxistes! Far from overcoming romantic sentimentality, the sociological critics just substituted a different kind of sentimentality. The Formalists took utter delight in rejecting anything remotely spiritual, ethical, or otherwise "uplifting" as so much unscientific bosh.

Bloodless Blood

Whatever makes literature literary, then, it could not be any of those questions Tolstoy had in mind when he titled a story "What People Live By." Nothing could be less scientific than "the meaning of life," the nature of right and wrong, or problems of good and evil. Only philistines regard literature this way. As the Formalists liked to say, one might as well rush on to the stage to stay the hand of the actor playing Judas. Like so many scientistic reductionists, they took a rather unscientific delight in calling their opponents rubes.

Victor Shklovsky famously voices this insouciant nihilism on page 44 of the present collection: "Gore in art is not necessarily gory; it rhymes with *amor*." More literally, the line says: "Blood in art is not bloody; it rhymes with love" (in Russian, "blood" and "love" do rhyme). For Shklovsky, literary blood is entirely bloodless. Blood is simply "the substance of the tonal structure or material for the construction of figures of speech. Art, then, is unsympathetic—or beyond sympathy—except where the feeling of compassion is evoked as material for the artistic structure. In discussing such emotion we have to examine it from the point of view of the composition itself, in exactly the same way that a mechanic must examine a driving belt to understand the details of a machine."

The machine metaphor was of course designed to shock. Art is not inspiration but fabrication. The Formalists loved to use the word "make" (rather than "create"), especially in the title of articles, or to adopt industrial terms. Anything to discredit the reverential, romantic, or otherwise unscientific view of art as the product of unfathomable genius! For much the same reason, Shklovsky liked to use obscene jokes as examples of what was going on in acknowledged masterpieces.

It was statements like these that made Bakhtin argue that the Formalists themselves had missed the very essence of literature. As Bakhtin explained, they had fallen victim to, and relied for their appeal on, "a vogue for science, of superficial imitation of science, of a prematurely self-confident scientific tone where the time of real science has not yet come. For the striving to construct a science, at any cost and as quickly as possible, frequently leads to an extreme lowering of the level of problematics, to the impoverishment of the object under study, and even to the illegitimate replacement of this object—in this case, artistic creation—by something entirely different."[5]

Bakhtin attacked the Formalists on their central claim: to have developed an approach to literature based on "the object under study." That was precisely what they failed to do, Bakhtin contended. Bakhtin saw literature as "verbal art," and so, like all art, it constitutes a distinct (aesthetic) approach to the human condition. Artists and writers correctly insist that "their creative work is value-related, that it is directed toward the world, toward reality, that it has to do with human beings, with social relations, with ethical, religious and other values."[6]

Bakhtin, however, also found value in Formalist theories, and many of his best ideas rely on or recast Formalist insights. Where the Formalists identified a literary device (as they repeatedly do in this collection), Bakhtin sought to give an aesthetic explanation of its use in terms of the meanings and values it conveys. For Bakhtin, therefore, Formalism "is harmless and, given a methodically clear-cut awareness of the limits of its applicability, it can even be productive in studying *technique* in artistic creation. But it becomes unmitigatedly harmful and inadmissible when it is taken as a basis for understanding and studying artistic creativity as a whole."[7]

PETRIFYING THE STONE

If for the Formalists literature has nothing to do with meaning and value as Bakhtin understood these concepts, then what *is* the essence of literature in their view? Here the Formalists offered a series of brilliant answers. Most famously, they insisted that art is defined by what Shklovsky called "defamiliarization," or as the word is sometimes more literally rendered, "bestrangement" (*ostranenie*). The idea comes from learning theory. In ordinary life, as we learn to do something it becomes a habit. We no longer have to think of each muscular adjustment. If we had to fix our attention on everything that goes into walking or driving—as we did when these skills were being acquired—we could not do more than one thing at a time. Attention is a highly limited resource, and habit keeps our mental hands free, so to speak. The problem is that habit itself may block our perception—may lead us to forget the details of something familiar or overlook the new in something already habitualized. Instead of seeing things as we did when they were fresh, we merely *recognize* them. Sometimes that can lead us to miss what is most important.

To reverse this process of automatization, we need to make the familiar unfamiliar again—to "defamiliarize" or "bestrange" it. That is the task of art. Without art, Shklovsky famously argued, "life is reckoned as nothing. Habitualization devours works, clothes, furniture, one's wife, and the fear of war. . . . [A]rt exists that one may recover the sensation of life; it exists . . . to make the stone *stony*. The purpose of art is to impart the sensation of things as they are perceived and not as they are known" (12). Here we see the salvationist side of Formalism: Formalists, too, see art as having profound moral significance. Theirs is the ethic of the avant-garde, of the cultural revolutionary. Lives lived according to habit: "such lives are as if they had never been."

Then where do they differ from Bakhtin? To begin with, Bakhtin valued tradition as well as novelty. More important, the Formalists usually forgot the moral implications of their theory. Or they limited its application to art itself. The only perception they cared to see renewed was the perception of artistic forms themselves, a preference that explains why the Formalists especially loved what we have come to call metaliterature, like *Tristram Shandy*. They enthused about what they called "baring the device." A device is "bared" when it is not "motivated," that is, when the author overtly has a character do something not because the character wants or needs to but because that is what the conventions of art demand.

In short, art exists not to make the stone stony but to make the language of poetry poetic. Thus, in the very passage about defamiliarization I have just quoted, Shklovsky rather inconsistently concludes: "*Art is a way of experiencing the artfulness of an object; the object is not important*" (12, italics in original).

In his essay on *Tristram Shandy*, Shklovsky treats that self-conscious novel as concerned centrally with literary forms and conventions—an approach we now take for granted but then was quite new. Sterne was still often assumed to be a mere sentimentalist. Tolstoy valued him as a psychologist. But Shklovsky not only identifies the metaliterary aspects of *Tristram Shandy*, he denies the existence of any other. Everything else in the book is simply so much material for playing with forms. For Shklovsky, that is true of all literature, but Sterne makes this pure formalism explicit. That is how Shklovsky can arrive at a deliberately paradoxical conclusion about Sterne's idiosyncratic masterpiece: "*Tristram Shandy* is the most typical novel in world literature" (57). However atypical it is in the sense of uncommon, it is typical because it represents the essence of literature. Its content is form. It depicts not its characters but literariness itself.

WORDS BY THE POUND

As Formalism evolved, Eichenbaum and Boris Tomashevsky offered a more nuanced understanding of form and defamiliarization. Instead of opposing form to content, and denying the latter, they saw literariness as applying the shaping power of defamiliarization to extraliterary material. The opposite of form was no longer content but extraliterary *material*. That is why Bakhtin referred to Formalism as a branch of what he called "material aesthetics": it understands "artistic form as the form of a given material and nothing more."[8] Literature is words made palpably verbal.

It is hardly surprising, then, that so many Formalists were linguists or relied heavily on linguistics. Words were the material of art, and so it seemed that to be a scientist—and therefore a materialist—one had to reduce all of art to so many words. Of course, it is decidedly odd to claim the banner of materialism for words, which, after all, have neither mass nor extension, traditionally the defining attributes of matter. How much do metaphors weigh? But in abusing the prestige of materialism the Formalists are hardly unique. We could just as easily ask a Marxist: How much do "exploitation" or "feudalism" weigh?

Bakhtin noted that in reducing literary study to a branch of linguistics, the Formalists were contradicting their own requirement that the discipline must be based on the specifically literary. Linguistic reductionism was still reductionism.

ATOMISM AND PLOT

The Formalists added to this kind of "materialism" another, equally seductive, concept for would-be scientists: atomism. To such thinkers it seems as if a properly scientific approach first dismembers the object under investigation to its most primitive elements and then studies the ways these elements combine. That is precisely what the Formalists did with literature and many of its genres. Their contributions based on this way of thinking have retained lasting influence.

Consider their approach to plot, as demonstrated by Tomashevsky's essay in the present volume. Tomashevsky explains: "After reducing a work to its thematic elements, we come to parts that are irreducible, the smallest particles of thematic material: 'evening comes,' 'Raskolnikov kills the old woman,' 'the hero dies,' 'the letter is received,' and so on. The theme of an irreducible part of a work is called the *motif*" (67). Motifs combine to form a story, which is the sequence of events as they occur in temporal and causal order in real life. The author then forms this material into an artistic order in which the events are presented in an artistically effective way, which is to say, not in chronological order and, perhaps, with digressions.

Jakobson wrote that "poetic form is the organized coercion of language" (quoted in Eichenbaum, 127), that is, it is "practical" language deformed into poetic language. In much the same way, *plot* (*siuzhet*) may be regarded as organized coercion of *story* (*fabula*), that is, the real-life sequence is deformed into the artistic order we find in novels. As Tomashevsky puts it, "Real incidents, not fictionalized by an author, may make a story. A plot is wholly an artistic creation" (68).

Because authors often manipulate their presentation of events, Formalist insights led to numerous useful studies, many by the Formalists themselves. For folklorists, Vladimir Propp's studies of the plots of fairy tales retain enormous influence a century later. There is much to be said for this approach, but one may also detect a serious ambiguity.

Is the "story" that the author defamiliarizes the real sequence of events or is it rather the way we usually narrate those events? Shklovsky and Tomashevsky write as if we usually narrate events in chronological order and as if only an artist ever does something else. But a moment's thought will reveal that we rarely narrate any complex set of events in chronological order. If we are describing how two people came into conflict, we may trace the events experienced by one until he encounters the other, whose experiences we then go back to trace. We do not jump from one causal line to another in order to keep the chronological order. Indeed, so rarely do we keep to strict chronological order that to do so would itself be a form of defamiliarization.

We tell stories for a reason. When we narrate, we are trying to make ourselves understood so as to convey a point, and it is that point, not chronological order, that dictates how we narrate. The Formalists err because they forget real, lived human experience, which always comes with purposes, in order to focus on raw material and form, which do not.

GENRES

As Eichenbaum and Shklovsky explained, the Formalists approached longer genres from their atomistic perspective. Motifs combine into anecdotes, anecdotes into short stories, short stories into novels. The progression from shorter to longer forms is entirely a matter of devices. Thus, Shklovsky explained that writers first learned to combine stories by using a frame narrative about how people told a sequence of stories, as in the *Decameron* or the *Canterbury Tales.* Then they got the idea of making the stories all the adventures of a single hero. The reason that Don Quixote appears to be both noble and foolish, according to Shklovsky, is not that the book examines the complexity of idealism but that Cervantes used linking devices that did not (as in later novels) presuppose a consistent hero. "The type of Don Quixote, so glorified by Heine and beslobbered by Turgenev, was not the primary aim of the author. The type was the result of the process of constructing the novel, just as the mechanism of performance often creates new forms of poetry."[9]

The Bakhtin group took the Formalists to task for such conclusions, which were to them evidently absurd. The Formalists' core error, they contended, lay in their misunderstanding of *genre.* Formalist atomism notwithstanding, a genre is not a particular complex of devices assembled from the bottom up. On the contrary, a genre is a particular way of understanding and evaluating some aspect of life. It proceeds from the top down, that is, from its perception of the world to its means of expression.

For the Bakhtin group, a genre has "eyes." Different genres see and evaluate the world differently. Realist novels are not just long anecdotes, because the "anecdotal" view of life differs markedly from the novelistic one. Nor do all long narratives—"novels" in the purely formal sense of the term—express the same view. Realist works like *Middlemarch* or *Anna Karenina* belong to an entirely different genre, and reflect a different way of viewing life, from *The Golden Ass, Pilgrim's Progress, Gulliver's Travels*, and *Moby-Dick*, all of which differ generically from each other. Genres are "form-shaping ideologies," by which Bakhtin meant they are ways of viewing the world that create or reshape appropriate forms to convey that view. Forms do not define a genre; they result from the vision that does. This debate—between atomists and what we might call "visionists"—continues.

The Formalists tried to rescue literature from reductionist approaches that did not reflect its integrity and complexity. If they sometimes went overboard in separating literature from life, they nevertheless left us an excellent set of analytic tools. As Bakhtin would be the first to acknowledge, no school of criticism can afford to ignore the Formalists' contributions.

NOTES

1. I capitalize "Formalism" and "Formalist" when referring specifically to Russian Formalism. There have been many movements that have been called, for one reason or another, formalist, and the term (with a small "f") is often used to refer to this approach as a whole.

2. The Bakhtin circle's two most important examinations of Formalism are Mikhail Bakhtin, "The Problem of Content, Material, and Form in Verbal Art," in *Art and Answerability: Early Philosophical Essays*, trans. Vadim Liapunov, ed. Michael Holquist and Vadim Liapunov (Austin: University of Texas Press, 1990), 276–325; and P. N. Medvedev, *The Formal Method in Literary Scholarship: A Critical Introduction to Sociological Poetics*, trans. Albert J. Wehrle (Cambridge MA: Harvard University Press, 1985). For a more detailed discussion of Bakhtin's and Medvedev's critique of Formalist theories of genre, see Gary Saul Morson and Caryl Emerson, *Mikhail Bakhtin: Creation of a Prosaics* (Stanford: Stanford University Press, 1990), 271–305. The best study of the Formalist movement is still the classic one by Victor Erlich, which has gone through numerous

editions and printings and has provided a model for studies of other movements. See Victor Erlich, *Russian Formalism: History—Doctrine* (New Haven: Yale University Press, 1981).

3. Gary S. Becker, *The Economic Approach to Human Behavior* (Chicago: University of Chicago Press, 1978), 14.

4. For an account of these origins of economics, see Stephen Toulmin, "Economics, or the Physics That Never Was," in *Return to Reason* (Cambridge MA: Harvard University Press, 2001), 47–66.

5. Bakhtin, "The Problem of Content," 258.

6. Bakhtin, "The Problem of Content," 262.

7. Bakhtin, "The Problem of Content," 263.

8. Bakhtin, "The Problem of Content," 262.

9. Quoted in Medvedev, *The Formal Method in Literary Scholarship*, 136.

Contents

Introduction

Despite the serious attention given Slavic Formalist literary criticism in René Wellek and Austin Warren's *Theory of Literature*[1] and Victor Erlich's thorough study of the Russian branch,[2] readers of English have had little chance to examine the works themselves. Historically, the fact that during the 1920's a group of Russian critics urged the separation of literature and politics challenges our popular clichés about Soviet control of literary theory, and the fact that the group was "disciplined" about 1930 confirms them. But this is just a part of the long and complex story of unorthodox views in the Soviet Union, and cannot be pursued here. Our topic is the internal history of the movement and the theory it developed.

An English-speaking reader going through the early works of the Formalists will often feel that, despite differences of names and details of argument, he is on familiar ground. With the necessary adjustments, he recognizes some of the concepts of the New Critics, their strategies, and even their enemies. Both the Russian and the Anglo-American movements began brashly by assuming that the traditional academic approaches to literature were invalid because they avoided literature. T. E. Hulme, who caught the spirit of the New Critics long before they were given a name, chided poets for their eagerness to jump impulsively from poems into the infinite,[3]

1. René Wellek and Austin Warren, *Theory of Literature* (New York: Harcourt, Brace & Co., 1949), introduction to Pt. IV, and Chaps. 13 and 16.

2. Victor Erlich, *Russian Formalism: History-Doctrine* (Vol. IV in *Slavistic Printings and Reprintings*, ed. Cornelis H. Van Schooneveld; 'S-Gravenhage: Mouton & Co., 1955).

We are heavily indebted to Mr. Erlich's fine pioneering study, both because it stimulated our initial interest in Russian Formalism and because, when well into our work, we found that he had done his job so expertly that our introductory material could do little more than summarize what he had found.

3. T. E. Hulme, *Speculations: Essays on Humanism and the Philosophy of Art*, ed. Herbert Read (New York: Harcourt, Brace & Co., 1936), p. 116.

much as John Crowe Ransom later attacked literary scholars who, with the very slightest provocation, would jump eagerly from literature into anything. As a result, Ransom argued, literary study had no discipline; the professional student of literature played historian, philosopher, or social reformer.[4] The strategy of the New Critics—arrived at not by concerted deliberation but by chance and mutual interest—involved three related activities: (1) the mounting of an attack against traditional academic scholarship; (2) the development of a critical theory which would separate literature from history, sociology, and philosophy; and (3) the creation of a way of talking about literary works that would replace discussions of background, social usefulness, or intellectual content with analysis of structure.

The Formalists' strategy paralleled that of the New Critics. They first attacked previous scholarship and defended aggressively the narrow limits they imposed upon literary study. Earlier Russian literary scholars, like their British and American counterparts at the turn of the century, had enjoyed such freedom in their discipline that they found themselves with no discipline. The scholarship generally followed one of three retreats from literature: the historical, which studied literary backgrounds but often ignored the literature itself; the moral-social, which treated literature as an instrument for the ethical and social betterment of man; and the philological, which included historical and linguistic studies in folklore and comparative literature. The Russian Formalists, like the New Critics, learned much from the teachers whose works they were forced to attack. Historical scholarship had made extensive and precise information easily available; indeed, the Formalists' work depended upon the availability of a huge reservoir of historical data. The moral-social critics like Vissarion Belinsky, Nicholas Chernyshevsky, Nicholas Dobroliubov, and Dmitry Pisarev contributed indirectly and negatively. Their position in relation to the Formalists is like that of the Matthew Arnold–Paul Elmer More axis in relation to the New Critics: their judgments were generally considered irrelevant because they expected the wrong things of literature and because

4. John Crowe Ransom, *The World's Body* (New York: Charles Scribner's Sons, 1938), pp. 326–329.

they attempted to judge the "message" of literary works without first considering specifically literary problems.

But the Formalists learned most from the philologists—from Alexander Potebnya (1835–1891) and Alexander Veselovsky (1838–1906). Each in his own way worked toward a distinctly literary study of literature; each contributed to the discovery of an approach to literature that would prevent its subservience to any and all other disciplines. Potebnya's insight was one of those simple discoveries that, when proclaimed, inevitably lead to a revolution in thought. Following Wilhelm von Humboldt, Potebnya saw poetry and prose (aesthetic and nonaesthetic language) as distinct, as separate approaches to the understanding of reality linked by their dependence upon language. Like many British and American critics of the following century, he drew two basic conclusions from this insight: that the study of literature as literature must be primarily a study of language, and that the preliminary problem in such a study is to define the peculiarities of poetic language as opposed to prose or practical-scientific language. This initial problem was also the starting point for I. A. Richards in books like *Principles of Literary Criticism* and *Science and Poetry*.

But the paths taken by the New Critics and Potebnya diverged sharply. Those New Critics influenced by Richards preferred to characterize poetry as discourse (pseudo statement or suprascientific statement, depending upon the critic) made unusually complex and compact. The weakness of the New Criticism, at least in its early stages, was its almost exclusively semantic orientation. Potebnya avoided that weakness and fell into another; instead of irony, he made metaphor the basis of all poetry. But as Victor Shklovsky points out in "Art as Technique" (see pp. 5–6), Potebnya's metaphors work in only one direction: they work only by presenting the unknown in terms of the known. Thus for Potebnya metaphor is essentially an aid to understanding, and poetry, the particular example of a general truth. Potebnya's work was much more subtle than this; but the course of Russian poetry and criticism in the first two decades of the twentieth century led to the simplification, and it was the simplification that the Formalists felt they had to attack.

Positively, however, Potebnya had defined one approach to a

purely literary study of literature. If the distinguishing characteristic of literature is the way it uses words, then the job of the student of literature is to study the way words are used. This was the earliest concern of the Formalists.

Veselovsky's contribution to Formalism is different from Potebnya's, and its basis less familiar to Western literary critics. Having arrived by a long and difficult process at the conclusion that the study of literature had to be self-contained—that it could not legitimately overlap into other disciplines—he argued that the motif and its uses were the proper subjects of literary study. A motif, as the term came to be used, is any simple unit entering into a work of art; as we see in "Thematics" (see pp. 67–75), a skilled and logical critic like Boris Tomashevsky can use the concept of the motif to explain much about the structure of literary works. Perhaps the only things comparable to Veselovsky's work in American criticism are the studies of motifs in folklore [5] (folklore also provided the basis for a great deal of Veselovsky's research) and the considerably less schematic and less generalized practical criticism of R. S. Crane and the Chicago school. The latter's concern with the internal determination of the work of art, the justification of detail in terms of structure, can be roughly translated into the kind of motif study the Formalists developed from Veselovsky's work.

Potebnya and Veselovsky, then, were the scholars from whom the Russian Formalists learned most. They were also strongly influenced by the direction Russian poetry took during the opening decades of the twentieth century, in particular by the struggle between the Russian Symbolists, whose literary theory was based largely on Potebnya's, and the Futurists. Both groups had vocal spokesmen eager to engage in the journalistic polemics that Boris Eichenbaum describes in "The Theory of the 'Formal Method'" (see pp. 103–106).

If we can imagine a continuing debate between Shelley and T. E.

---

5. Particularly relevant are the approaches used by Stith Thompson in *Motif-Index of Folk Literature* (rev. ed.; Bloomington: Indiana University Press, 1955), and Antti Aarne, *The Types of Folktale*, trans. and enlarged by Stith Thompson (Folklore Fellows Communication No. 184; Helsinki: Suomalainen Tiedeakatemia Academia Scientiarum Fennica, 1961).

Hulme, the former defending his idealistic, mellifluous verse and the latter arguing for poetry that is "all dry and hard,"[6] then we have something like the issues involved in the debate between the Symbolists and the Futurists. The Symbolists, led by Vyacheslav Ivanov, Alexander Blok, Andrey Bely, Valery Bryusov, and Konstantin Balmont argued that poetry is the expression of a higher reality; the tone of their critical theory can be indicated briefly by the title of Balmont's book *Poetry as Magic.*[7] This view of poetry as mystic, and as a mystique, was probably the chief factor in alienating the Formalists from the Symbolists, although the bulk of the Formalist attacks concern technique. The high claims for poetry to which the Formalists objected were, in fact, indirectly responsible for much of the content of early Formalist criticism. Because the Symbolists took poetry so seriously, some of the members of the group were also willing to examine it technically. Bely and Bryusov in particular saw that if poetry were really to express the ultimate, then everything about the poem was important. If the poem is a microcosm of the universe, then its details—metrics, pitch patterns, all the minutiae of prosody—are significant. Or, to use the metaphor that we have become used to since Coleridge, in an organic form even the most minute organs function. As a result, Bely and Bryusov were especially interested in developing a Symbolist theory of prosody.[8] The Formalists attacked their theory.

An example of the practical differences between the two groups might clarify matters. The Symbolists were much concerned with onomatopoeia because in the vast system of correspondences between word and physical reality, and between physical and spiritual reality that they conceived, onomatopoeia seemed a clear instance of a thing on one level (sound) corresponding with something on another level (physical or perhaps emotional reality). The Formalists disagreed, preferring to argue either that the effects of onomatopoeia were exaggerated or illusionary, or that the sound of poetry is interesting enough in itself to require no further justification. The

6. Hulme, *Speculations*, p. 126.

7. Konstantin Balmont, *Poeziya kak volshebstvo* (Moscow, 1915), cited by Erlich, *Russian Formalism*, p. 19.

8. Especially in Andrey Bely's *Simvolizm* [*Symbolism*] (Moscow, 1910).

Formalists also felt that before entering into such murky theoretical areas as the relationship between sound and meaning they should first determine the facts of literature—how do poets actually use rhyme, rhythm, the tonal properties of vowels and consonants, and so on? To answer these questions, they had to seal off their subject from ethics, sociology, philosophy, psychology, and what have you until they attained a precise and detailed knowledge of what actually happens within literary works.

Eichenbaum, who was less personally involved with the Futurists than were the other early Formalists, suggests that the Formalists and the Futurists joined forces because they had a common enemy—Symbolism. Actually, there were other reasons, some personal and some theoretical. Vladimir Mayakovsky, one of the most articulate of the Futurist spokesmen, frequented the informal gatherings from which the *Opoyaz*[9] (the name taken by the Petersburg Formalists) grew. Theoretically, the Futurists, denying the notion of symbolic correspondence, were left with a notion of poetry as a thing valuable in itself. The Futurists, like the Formalists, were interested in poetic devices not as bearers of meaning, but as details with intrinsic value; in short, both groups were quite narrowly interested in poetry as poetry.

Such, then, is the general background from which the Formalists emerged. We shall not trace the development of the movement, since Eichenbaum's "The Theory of the 'Formal Method'" (see pp. 99 ff.) does that brilliantly. The reader wanting still more extensive information will find it in Erlich's *Russian Formalism: History-Doctrine*; the theories of the Formalists are also discussed helpfully in Wellek and Warren's *Theory of Literature* and in Wellek's *Concepts of Criticism*.[10]

9. *Opoyaz* comes from *Obschestvo izucheniya poeticheskovo yazyka* (Society for the Study of Poetic Language). This was the name taken by the Petersburg Formalists, a group which included Victor Shklovsky, Leo Jakubinsky, and Boris Eichenbaum. The Moscow group, called the Moscow Linguistic Circle, was led in part by Roman Jakobson; early contributors to its meetings included Osip Brik and Boris Tomashevsky. The groups were allies rather than rivals, and Eichenbaum does not distinguish between them. The first official publication, in 1916, of the *Opoyaz* was the *Sborniki po teorii poeticheskovo yazyka* [*Studies in the Theory of Poetic Language*], hereafter referred to as *Sborniki*.

10. René Wellek, *Concepts of Criticism* (New Haven: Yale University Press, 1963).

The suppression of the movement deserves a note. The fact that Formalism, superficially a purely aesthetic approach to literature, flourished in Russia during the early years of the Soviet Union should occasion less surprise than it does. Revolutionary movements tend to be idealistic and confused before they become established. Revolutions waged in the name of freedom tend, at least briefly, to be rather permissive. Moreover, immediately after the Revolution, Russian officials had more pressing business than the future of poetry. Because the Formalists were not directly engaged in ideological battles, they could be ignored until the general attitude of the Soviet government towards literature could be formulated. By the late 1920's the official attitude had hardened; the extreme Marxist literary groups that had unofficially and then semiofficially harassed the Formalists now attacked them officially and viciously. Victor Erlich has chronicled the story in some detail.[11]

With the death of Formalism, the leading Formalists turned to work more in keeping with Soviet orthodoxy. Boris Eichenbaum continued his work on Tolstoy; Shklovsky studied Tolstoy and Mayakovsky (both "approved" officially) and, like other Formalists, devoted increasing attention to the movies and to contemporary literature.

The major exception is Roman Jakobson, who left the Moscow Linguistic Circle in 1920 to continue his work in Prague. By the time the Prague Linguistic Circle had coalesced into a relatively stable group (in 1926), Jakobson was recognized as one of its leading members. The Moscow group had been interested chiefly in literature, with a strong secondary interest in linguistics; the Prague group, which included René Wellek, was interested chiefly in linguistics, with a strong secondary interest in literature. Jakobson, armed with the concepts developed during his participation in the Moscow meetings, was in a position to take a leading role in Prague. The similarity of the concepts of the two groups is perhaps shown best by the fact that Eichenbaum, in his survey of Jakobson's work in "The Theory of the 'Formal Method,'" makes no distinction between Jakobson's studies at Moscow and his studies at Prague.

11. Erlich, *Russian Formalism*, Chaps. VI and VII.

Although the detour was long, the methods of the Prague School—
if not all of their conclusions—are beginning to find their way into
American poetics. The work of such linguists and critics as Archibald
Hill, Seymour Chatman, Dwight Bollinger, George L. Trager and
H. L. Smith Jr., and Harold Whitehall (to name only a few) con-
tinue the line of study established by the Russian Formalists and the
Prague Linguists.

A Note on the Text

The essays presented here have, we believe, a special interest for
readers who know no Russian. They not only illustrate the principles
of Russian Formalism and show their practical applications, they
also rely heavily on examples familiar to the English-speaking
reader. The selection was approved by Victor Shklovsky, who
perhaps more than anyone else deserves to be called the founder of
Russian Formalism.

Unfortunately, some important work had to be omitted. Roman
Jakobson's extremely valuable contributions to Slavic Formalism
are omitted because he is carrying on his work in English in the
United States. We have also regretfully omitted the work of such
important theoreticians as Leo Jakubinsky and Victor Zhirmunsky
because their chief contributions are highly technical studies of
Russian prosody; such work, despite its merit, does not bear
translation well.

In editing the following selections, we have generally tried to be
as sparing as possible in the use of footnotes, limiting them chiefly
to notes supplied in the original and to those necessary to clarify the
text or to draw parallels between Russian and Western criticism.
We have avoided the temptation to supply information about the
numerous writers and movements cited in the original texts, even
though these are likely to be unfamiliar to the general reader, unless
their pertinence to the text is not clear.

We have, where practicable, normalized the varying note styles
of the authors without indicating the changes. Significant additions
to the original notes are in brackets; the editors' notes are marked.
All Russian titles have been transliterated, except those with well-

established English translations. Where authors have cited works originally in English, we have quoted the English text.

Except where otherwise indicated, we have provided the translations of passages quoted from various Russian texts in the original essays. Foreign words and phrases have also been translated in the text, with the bracketed original form following the English translation.

LEE T. LEMON
University of Nebraska

MARION J. REIS
*Oak Park and River Forest
High School*

VICTOR SHKLOVSKY

Art as Technique

Victor Shklovsky is certainly the most erratic and probably the most important of the Formalist critics. A charter member of the group, he had that rare combination of brilliant originality, combativeness, and theoretical flexibility required of a propagandist during the early years of a movement. As Eichenbaum shows ("The Theory of the 'Formal Method'"), Shklovsky touched most of the fundamentals of Formalist theory, was often the first to define a problem, and frequently pointed towards its solution. He saw issues clearly and stated them sharply—perhaps too sharply. Like T. E. Hulme or T. S. Eliot, he was a master of the kind of statement that disciples make slogans of and opponents find embarrassingly easy to attack. Because he was the most obvious and the most vulnerable target for the Marxists and because his attitude toward the Russian Revolution was unusually complex,[1] he was one of the first of the Formalists to attempt a compromise. By 1926 he was trying to include sociological material in his study of literature; his work on Tolstoy in 1928 analyzes War and Peace *as a product of two irreconcilable forces—the social class Tolstoy represented and the novel as a genre.[2]*

"Art as Technique" (1917) is the most important statement made of early Formalist method, partly because it announces a break with the only other "aesthetic" approach available at that time and in that place, and partly because it offers a theory of both the methodology of criticism and the purpose of art. Although we have discussed the Formalists' quarrel with Potebnya in general terms, more specific comment is appropriate here. Shklovsky attacks the views, both typical of Potebnyaism, that "art is thinking in images" and that its purpose is to present the unknown (most often the abstract or transcendent) in terms of the known. Theoretically, the views recognized neither the richness

1. Victor Erlich, *Russian Formalism: History-Doctrine* (Vol. IV of *Slavistic Printings and Reprintings*, ed. Cornelis H. Van Schooneveld; 'S-Gravenhage: Mouton & Co., 1955), pp. 112–114.

2. Victor Shklovsky, "*Voyna i mir* Lva Tolstovo (Formalno-sotsiologicheskoye issledovaniye)" ["*War and Peace* of Leo Tolstoy (A Formalistic-Sociological Study)"], *Novy lef* [*New Left*], No. 1 (1928).

of poetry nor its intrinsic value. Empirically, the views were inadequate, as Shklovsky points out. To use an example from Wordsworth, the lines

> The world is too much with us; late and soon,
> Getting and spending, we lay waste our powers:

are certainly poetic, yet it would be rash to argue that the poetic quality comes from the deeply latent imagery. And at the end of his sonnet, Wordsworth resurrects Proteus and Triton as images to evoke a feeling that many persons have had first hand; the image here is less familiar than the thing it stands for. The Potebnya-Symbolist description of poetry, then, was inadequate both theoretically and practically.

At this time the Formalists needed a critical formula that would define the difference between literature and non-literature more precisely and more generally than had been done, and that would at the same time state the purpose of literature. Shklovsky's concept of "defamiliarization" [3] did both. It was appropriate historically, since, in effect, it simply turned Potebnyaism upside down. Shklovsky's argument, briefly stated, is that the habitual way of thinking is to make the unfamiliar as easily digestible as possible. Normally our preceptions are "automatic," which is another way of saying that they are minimal. From this standpoint, learning is largely a matter of learning to ignore. We have not really learned to drive an automobile, for example, until we are able to react to the relevant stoplights, pedestrians, other motorists, road conditions, and so on, with a minimum of conscious effort. Eventually, we may even react properly without actually noticing what we are reacting to—we miss the pedestrian but fail to see what he looks like. When reading ordinary prose, we are likely to feel that something is wrong if we find ourselves noticing the individual words as words. The purpose of art, according to Shklovsky, is to force us to notice. Since perception is usually too automatic, art develops a variety of techniques to impede perception or, at least, to call attention to themselves. Thus "Art is a way of experiencing the artfulness of an object; the object is not important." [4] *The object is unimportant because as art the poem does not have to point to anything outside itself; the poem must "not mean/But be."*

This is not the place to debate the merits of conflicting aesthetic systems, but we should note that Shklovsky's position is more subtle than its opponents

3. The Russian word is *ostraneniye*; it means literally "making strange."
4. See below, p. 12.

would admit. To the extent that a work of art can be experienced, to the extent that it is, it is like any other object. It may "mean" in the same way that any object means; it has, however, one advantage—it is designed especially for perception, for attracting and holding attention. Thus it not only bears meaning, it forces an awareness of its meaning upon the reader. Although Shklovsky did not follow this line, it does widen the range of his theory without inconsistency. He prefers to argue, as does I. A. Richards, that perception is an end in itself, that the good life is the life of a man fully aware of the world. Art, to paraphrase Richards and to summarize Shklovsky, is the record of and the occasion for that awareness.[5]

According to Shklovsky, the chief technique for promoting such perception is "defamiliarization." It is not so much a device as a result obtainable by any number of devices. A novel point of view, as Shklovsky points out, can make a reader perceive by making the familiar seem strange. Wordplay, deliberately roughened rhythm, or figures of speech can all have the same effect. No single device, then, is essential to poetry. Poetry is recognized not by the presence of a certain kind of content or of images, ambiguities, symbols, or whatever, but by its ability to make man look with an exceptionally high level of awareness.

"Art is thinking in images." This maxim, which even high school students parrot, is nevertheless the starting point for the erudite philologist who is beginning to put together some kind of systematic literary theory. The idea, originated in part by Potebnya, has spread. "Without imagery there is no art, and in particular no poetry," Potebnya writes.[6] And elsewhere, "Poetry, as well as prose, is first and foremost a special way of thinking and knowing."[7]

Poetry is a special way of thinking; it is, precisely, a way of thinking in images, a way which permits what is generally called "economy of mental effort," a way which makes for "a sensation of the relative ease of the process." Aesthetic feeling is the reaction to

5. I. A. Richards, *Science and Poetry* (1926), reprinted in *Criticism: The Foundations of Modern Literary Judgment*, ed. Mark Schorer, Josephine Miles, and Gordon McKenzie (New York: Harcourt, Brace & Co., 1958), p. 513.

6. Alexander Potebnya, *Iz zapisok po teorii slovesnosti* [*Notes on the Theory of Language*] (Kharkov, 1905), p. 83.

7. *Ibid.*, p. 97.

this economy. This is how the academician Ovsyaniko-Kulikovsky,[8] who undoubtedly read the works of Potebnya attentively, almost certainly understood and faithfully summarized the ideas of his teacher. Potebnya and his numerous disciples consider poetry a special kind of thinking—thinking by means of images; they feel that the purpose of imagery is to help channel various objects and activities into groups and to clarify the unknown by means of the known. Or, as Potebnya wrote:

> The relationship of the image to what is being clarified is that: (a) the image is the fixed predicate of that which undergoes change—the unchanging means of attracting what is perceived as changeable. . . . (b) the image is far clearer and simpler than what it clarifies.[9]

In other words:

> Since the purpose of imagery is to remind us, by approximation, of those meanings for which the image stands, and since, apart from this, imagery is unnecessary for thought, we must be more familiar with the image than with what it clarifies.[10]

It would be instructive to try to apply this principle to Tyutchev's comparison of summer lightning to deaf and dumb demons or to Gogol's comparison of the sky to the garment of God.[11]

"Without imagery there is no art"—"Art is thinking in images." These maxims have led to far-fetched interpretations of individual works of art. Attempts have been made to evaluate even music, architecture, and lyric poetry as imagistic thought. After a quarter of a century of such attempts Ovsyaniko-Kulikovsky finally had to assign lyric poetry, architecture, and music to a special category of

8. Dmitry Ovsyaniko-Kulikovsky (1835–1920), a leading Russian scholar, was an early contributor to Marxist periodicals and a literary conservative, antagonistic towards the deliberately meaningless poems of the Futurists. *Ed. note.*

9. Potebnya, *Iz zapisok po teorii slovesnosti*, p. 314.

10. *Ibid.*, p. 291.

11. Fyodor Tyutchev (1803–1873), a poet, and Nicholas Gogol (1809–1852), a master of prose fiction and satire, are mentioned here because their bold use of imagery cannot be accounted for by Potebnya's theory. Shklovsky is arguing that writers frequently gain their effects by comparing the commonplace to the exceptional rather than vice versa. *Ed. note.*

imageless art and to define them as lyric arts appealing directly to the emotions. And thus he admitted an enormous area of art which is not a mode of thought. A part of this area, lyric poetry (narrowly considered), is quite like the visual arts; it is also verbal. But, much more important, visual art passes quite imperceptibly into nonvisual art; yet our perceptions of both are similar.

Nevertheless, the definition "Art is thinking in images," which means (I omit the usual middle terms of the argument) that art is the making of symbols, has survived the downfall of the theory which supported it. It survives chiefly in the wake of Symbolism, especially among the theorists of the Symbolist movement.

Many still believe, then, that thinking in images—thinking in specific scenes of "roads and landscape" and "furrows and boundaries" [12]—is the chief characteristic of poetry. Consequently, they should have expected the history of "imagistic art," as they call it, to consist of a history of changes in imagery. But we find that images change little; from century to century, from nation to nation, from poet to poet, they flow on without changing. Images belong to no one: they are "the Lord's." The more you understand an age, the more convinced you become that the images a given poet used and which you thought his own were taken almost unchanged from another poet. The works of poets are classified or grouped according to the new techniques that poets discover and share, and according to their arrangement and development of the resources of language; poets are much more concerned with arranging images than with creating them. Images are given to poets; the ability to remember them is far more important than the ability to create them.

Imagistic thought does not, in any case, include all the aspects of art nor even all the aspects of verbal art. A change in imagery is not essential to the development of poetry. We know that frequently an expression is thought to be poetic, to be created for aesthetic pleasure, although actually it was created without such intent—e.g., Annensky's opinion that the Slavic languages are especially poetic and Andrey Bely's ecstasy over the technique of placing adjectives after nouns, a technique used by eighteenth-century Russian poets.

12. This is an allusion to Vyacheslav Ivanov's *Borozdy i mezhi* [*Furrows and Boundaries*] (Moscow, 1916), a major statement of Symbolist theory. *Ed. note.*

Bely joyfully accepts the technique as something artistic, or more exactly, as intended, if we consider intention as art. Actually, this reversal of the usual adjective-noun order is a peculiarity of the language (which had been influenced by Church Slavonic). Thus a work may be (1) intended as prosaic and accepted as poetic, or (2) intended as poetic and accepted as prosaic. This suggests that the artistry attributed to a given work results from the way we perceive it. By "works of art," in the narrow sense, we mean works created by special techniques designed to make the works as obviously artistic as possible.

Potebnya's conclusion, which can be formulated "poetry equals imagery," gave rise to the whole theory that "imagery equals symbolism," that the image may serve as the invariable predicate of various subjects. (This conclusion, because it expressed ideas similar to the theories of the Symbolists, intrigued some of their leading representatives—Andrey Bely, Merezhkovsky and his "eternal companions" and, in fact, formed the basis of the theory of Symbolism.) The conclusion stems partly from the fact that Potebnya did not distinguish between the language of poetry and the language of prose. Consequently, he ignored the fact that there are two aspects of imagery: imagery as a practical means of thinking, as a means of placing objects within categories; and imagery as poetic, as a means of reinforcing an impression. I shall clarify with an example. I want to attract the attention of a young child who is eating bread and butter and getting the butter on her fingers. I call, "Hey, butterfingers!" This is a figure of speech, a clearly prosaic trope. Now a different example. The child is playing with my glasses and drops them. I call, "Hey, butterfingers!"[13] This figure of speech is a poetic trope. (In the first example, "butterfingers" is metonymic; in the second, metaphoric—but this is not what I want to stress.)

Poetic imagery is a means of creating the strongest possible impression. As a method it is, depending upon its purpose, neither more nor less effective than other poetic techniques; it is neither more nor less effective than ordinary or negative parallelism, com-

13. The Russian text involves a play on the word for "hat," colloquial for "clod," "duffer," etc. *Ed. note.*

parison, repetition, balanced structure, hyperbole, the commonly accepted rhetorical figures, and all those methods which emphasize the emotional effect of an expression (including words or even articulated sounds).[14] But poetic imagery only externally resembles either the stock imagery of fables and ballads or thinking in images— e.g., the example in Ovsyaniko-Kulikovsky's *Language and Art* in which a little girl calls a ball a little watermelon. Poetic imagery is but one of the devices of poetic language. Prose imagery is a means of abstraction: a little watermelon instead of a lampshade, or a little watermelon instead of a head, is only the abstraction of one of the object's characteristics, that of roundness. It is no different from saying that the head and the melon are both round. This is what is meant, but it has nothing to do with poetry.

The law of the economy of creative effort is also generally accepted. [Herbert] Spencer wrote:

> On seeking for some clue to the law underlying these current maxims, we may see shadowed forth in many of them, the importance of economizing the reader's or the hearer's attention. To so present ideas that they may be apprehended with the least possible mental effort, is the desideratum towards which most of the rules above quoted point. . . . Hence, carrying out the metaphor that language is the vehicle of thought, there seems reason to think that in all cases the friction and inertia of the vehicle deduct from its efficiency; and that in composition, the chief, if not the sole thing to be done, is to reduce this friction and inertia to the smallest possible amount.[15]

And R[ichard] Avenarius:

> If a soul possess inexhaustible strength, then, of course, it would be indifferent to how much might be spent from this inexhaustible source;

14. Shklovsky is here doing two things of major theoretical importance: (1) he argues that different techniques serve a single function, and that (2) no single technique is all-important. The second permits the Formalists to be concerned with any and all literary devices; the first permits them to discuss the devices from a single consistent theoretical position. *Ed. note.*

15. Herbert Spencer, *The Philosophy of Style* [(Humboldt Library, Vol. XXXIV; New York, 1882), pp. 2–3. Shklovsky's quoted reference, in Russian, preserves the idea of the original but shortens it].

only the necessarily expended time would be important. But since its forces are limited, one is led to expect that the soul hastens to carry out the apperceptive process as expediently as possible—that is, with comparatively the least expenditure of energy, and, hence, with comparatively the best result.

Petrazhitsky, with only one reference to the general law of mental effort, rejects [William] James's theory of the physical basis of emotion, a theory which contradicts his own. Even Alexander Veselovsky acknowledged the principle of the economy of creative effort, a theory especially appealing in the study of rhythm, and agreed with Spencer: "A satisfactory style is precisely that style which delivers the greatest amount of thought in the fewest words." And Andrey Bely, despite the fact that in his better pages he gave numerous examples of "roughened" rhythm [16] and (particularly in the examples from Baratynsky) showed the difficulties inherent in poetic epithets, also thought it necessary to speak of the law of the economy of creative effort in his book [17]—a heroic effort to create a theory of art based on unverified facts from antiquated sources, on his vast knowledge of the techniques of poetic creativity, and on Krayevich's high school physics text.

These ideas about the economy of energy, as well as about the law and aim of creativity, are perhaps true in their application to "practical" language; they were, however, extended to poetic language. Hence they do not distinguish properly between the laws of practical language and the laws of poetic language. The fact that Japanese poetry has sounds not found in conversational Japanese was hardly the first factual indication of the differences between poetic and everyday language. Leo Jakubinsky has observed that the law of the dissimilation of liquid sounds does not apply to poetic language. [18] This suggested to him that poetic language tolerated the admission of hard-to-pronounce conglomerations of similar sounds.

16. The Russian *zatrudyonny* means "made difficult." The suggestion is that poems with "easy" or smooth rhythms slip by unnoticed; poems that are difficult or "roughened" force the reader to attend to them. *Ed. note.*

17. *Simvolizm*, probably. *Ed. note.*

18. Leo Jakubinsky, "O zvukakh poeticheskovo yazyka" ["On the Sounds of Poetic Language"], *Sborniki*, I (1916), p. 38.

In his article, one of the first examples of scientific criticism, he indicates inductively the contrast (I shall say more about this point later) between the laws of poetic language and the laws of practical language.[19]

We must, then, speak about the laws of expenditure and economy in poetic language not on the basis of an analogy with prose, but on the basis of the laws of poetic language.

If we start to examine the general laws of perception, we see that as perception becomes habitual, it becomes automatic. Thus, for example, all of our habits retreat into the area of the unconsciously automatic; if one remembers the sensations of holding a pen or of speaking in a foreign language for the first time and compares that with his feeling at performing the action for the ten thousandth time, he will agree with us. Such habituation explains the principles by which, in ordinary speech, we leave phrases unfinished and words half expressed. In this process, ideally realized in algebra, things are replaced by symbols. Complete words are not expressed in rapid speech; their initial sounds are barely perceived. Alexander Pogodin offers the example of a boy considering the sentence "The Swiss mountains are beautiful" in the form of a series of letters: T, S, m, a, b.[20]

This characteristic of thought not only suggests the method of algebra, but even prompts the choice of symbols (letters, especially initial letters). By this "algebraic" method of thought we apprehend objects only as shapes with imprecise extensions; we do not see them in their entirety but rather recognize them by their main characteristics. We see the object as though it were enveloped in a sack. We know what it is by its configuration, but we see only its silhouette. The object, perceived thus in the manner of prose perception, fades and does not leave even a first impression; ultimately even the essence of what it was is forgotten. Such perception explains why we

19. Leo Jakubinsky, "Skopleniye odinakovykh plavnykh v prakticheskom i poeticheskom yazykakh" ["The Accumulation of Identical Liquids in Practical and Poetic Language"], *Sborniki*, II (1917), pp. 13–21.

20. Alexander Pogodin, *Yazyk, kak tvorchestvo* [*Language as Art*] (Kharkov, 1913), p. 42. [The original sentence was in French, "*Les montaignes de la Suisse sont belles*," with the appropriate initials.]

fail to hear the prose word in its entirety (see Leo Jakubinsky's article[21]) and, hence, why (along with other slips of the tongue) we fail to pronounce it. The process of "algebrization," the over-automatization of an object, permits the greatest economy of perceptive effort. Either objects are assigned only one proper feature—a number, for example—or else they function as though by formula and do not even appear in cognition:

> I was cleaning a room and, meandering about, approached the divan and couldn't remember whether or not I had dusted it. Since these movements are habitual and unconscious, I could not remember and felt that it was impossible to remember—so that if I had dusted it and forgot—that is, had acted unconsciously, then it was the same as if I had not. If some conscious person had been watching, then the fact could be established. If, however, no one was looking, or looking on unconsciously, if the whole complex lives of many people go on unconsciously, then such lives are as if they had never been.[22]

And so life is reckoned as nothing. Habitualization devours works, clothes, furniture, one's wife, and the fear of war. "If the whole complex lives of many people go on unconsciously, then such lives are as if they had never been." And art exists that one may recover the sensation of life; it exists to make one feel things, to make the stone *stony*. The purpose of art is to impart the sensation of things as they are perceived and not as they are known. The technique of art is to make objects "unfamiliar," to make forms difficult, to increase the difficulty and length of perception because the process of perception is an aesthetic end in itself and must be prolonged. *Art is a way of experiencing the artfulness of an object; the object is not important.*

The range of poetic (artistic) work extends from the sensory to the cognitive, from poetry to prose, from the concrete to the abstract: from Cervantes' Don Quixote—scholastic and poor nobleman, half consciously bearing his humiliation in the court of the duke—to the broad but empty Don Quixote of Turgenev; from Charlemagne to the name "king" [in Russian "Charles" and "king" obviously derive from the same root, *korol*]. The meaning of a work broadens

21. Jakubinsky, *Sborniki*, I (1916).

22. Leo Tolstoy's *Diary*, entry dated February 29, 1897. [The date is transcribed incorrectly; it should read March 1, 1897.]

to the extent that artfulness and artistry diminish; thus a fable symbolizes more than a poem, and a proverb more than a fable. Consequently, the least self-contradictory part of Potebnya's theory is his treatment of the fable, which, from his point of view, he investigated thóroughly. But since his theory did not provide for "expressive" works of art, he could not finish his book. As we know, *Notes on the Theory of Literature* was published in 1905, thirteen years after Potebnya's death. Potebnya himself completed only the section on the fable.[23]

After we see an object several times, we begin to recognize it. The object is in front of us and we know about it, but we do not see it[24]— hence we cannot say anything significant about it. Art removes objects from the automatism of perception in several ways. Here I want to illustrate a way used repeatedly by Leo Tolstoy, that writer who, for Merezhkovsky at least, seems to present things as if he himself saw them, saw them in their entirety, and did not alter them.

Tolstoy makes the familiar seem strange by not naming the familiar object. He describes an object as if he were seeing it for the first time, an event as if it were happening for the first time. In describing something he avoids the accepted names of its parts and instead names corresponding parts of other objects. For example, in "Shame" Tolstoy "defamiliarizes" the idea of flogging in this way: "to strip people who have broken the law, to hurl them to the floor, and to rap on their bottoms with switches," and, after a few lines, "to lash about on the naked buttocks." Then he remarks:

> Just why precisely this stupid, savage means of causing pain and not any other—why not prick the shoulders or any part of the body with needles, squeeze the hands or the feet in a vise, or anything like that?

I apologize for this harsh example, but it is typical of Tolstoy's way of pricking the conscience. The familiar act of flogging is made unfamiliar both by the description and by the proposal to change its form without changing its nature. Tolstoy uses this technique of "defamiliarization" constantly. The narrator of "Kholstomer," for

23. Alexander Potebnya, *Iz lektsy po teorii slovesnosti* [*Lectures on the Theory of Language*] (Kharkov, 1914).

24. Victor Shklovsky, *Voskresheniye slova* [*The Resurrection of the Word*] (Petersburg, 1914).

example, is a horse, and it is the horse's point of view (rather than a person's) that makes the content of the story seem unfamiliar. Here is how the horse regards the institution of private property:

> I understood well what they said about whipping and Christianity. But then I was absolutely in the dark. What's the meaning of "his own," "his colt"? From these phrases I saw that people thought there was some sort of connection between me and the stable. At the time I simply could not understand the connection. Only much later, when they separated me from the other horses, did I begin to understand. But even then I simply could not see what it meant when they called me "man's property." The words "my horse" referred to me, a living horse, and seemed as strange to me as the words "my land," "my air," "my water."
>
> But the words made a strong impression on me. I thought about them constantly, and only after the most diverse experiences with people did I understand, finally, what they meant. They meant this: In life people are guided by words, not by deeds. It's not so much that they love the possibility of doing or not doing something as it is the possibility of speaking with words, agreed on among themselves, about various topics. Such are the words "my" and "mine," which they apply to different things, creatures, objects, and even to land, people, and horses. They agree that only one may say "mine" about this, that, or the other thing. And the one who says "mine" about the greatest number of things is, according to the game which they've agreed to among themselves, the one they consider the most happy. I don't know the point of all this, but it's true. For a long time I tried to explain it to myself in terms of some kind of real gain, but I had to reject that explanation because it was wrong.
>
> Many of those, for instance, who called me their own never rode on me—although others did. And so with those who fed me. Then again, the coachman, the veterinarians, and the outsiders in general treated me kindly, yet those who called me their own did not. In due time, having widened the scope of my observations, I satisfied myself that the notion "my," not only in relation to us horses, has no other basis than a narrow human instinct which is called a sense of or right to private property. A man says "this house is mine" and never lives in it; he only worries about its construction and upkeep. A merchant says "my shop," "my dry goods shop," for instance, and does not even wear clothes made from the better cloth he keeps in his own shop.

There are people who call a tract of land their own, but they never set eyes on it and never take a stroll on it. There are people who call others their own, yet never see them. And the whole relationship between them is that the so-called "owners" treat the others unjustly.

There are people who call women their own, or their "wives," but their women live with other men. And people strive not for the good in life, but for goods they can call their own.

I am now convinced that this is the essential difference between people and ourselves. And therefore, not even considering the other ways in which we are superior, but considering just this one virtue, we can bravely claim to stand higher than men on the ladder of living creatures. The actions of men, at least those with whom I have had dealings, are guided by *words*—ours, by deeds.

The horse is killed before the end of the story, but the manner of the narrative, its technique, does not change:

Much later they put Serpukhovsky's body, which had experienced the world, which had eaten and drunk, into the ground. They could profitably send neither his hide, nor his flesh, nor his bones anywhere.

But since his dead body, which had gone about in the world for twenty years, was a great burden to everyone, its burial was only a superfluous embarrassment for the people. For a long time no one had needed him; for a long time he had been a burden on all. But nevertheless, the dead who buried the dead found it necessary to dress this bloated body, which immediately began to rot, in a good uniform and good boots; to lay it in a good new coffin with new tassels at the four corners, then to place this new coffin in another of lead and ship it to Moscow; there to exhume ancient bones and at just that spot, to hide this putrefying body, swarming with maggots, in its new uniform and clean boots, and to cover it over completely with dirt.

Thus we see that at the end of the story Tolstoy continues to use the technique even though the motivation for it [the reason for its use] is gone.[25]

In *War and Peace* Tolstoy uses the same technique in describing whole battles as if battles were something new. These descriptions are too long to quote; it would be necessary to extract a considerable

25. See below, pp. 85–86, for a discussion of the motivational aspects of defamiliarization. *Ed. note.*

part of the four-volume novel. But Tolstoy uses the same method in describing the drawing room and the theater:

> The middle of the stage consisted of flat boards; by the sides stood painted pictures representing trees, and at the back a linen cloth was stretched down to the floor boards. Maidens in red bodices and white skirts sat on the middle of the stage. One, very fat, in a white silk dress, sat apart on a narrow bench to which a green pasteboard box was glued from behind. They were all singing something. Whey they had finished, the maiden in white approached the prompter's box. A man in silk with tight-fitting pants on his fat legs approached her with a plume and began to sing and spread his arms in dismay. The man in the tight pants finished his song alone; then the girl sang. After that both remained silent as the music resounded; and the man, obviously waiting to begin singing his part with her again, began to run his fingers over the hand of the girl in the white dress. They finished their song together, and everyone in the theater began to clap and shout. But the men and women on stage, who represented lovers, started to bow, smiling and raising their hands.
>
> In the second act there were pictures representing monuments and openings in the linen cloth representing the moonlight, and they raised lamp shades on a frame. As the musicians started to play the bass horn and counter-bass, a large number of people in black mantles poured onto the stage from right and left. The people, with something like daggers in their hands, started to wave their arms. Then still more people came running out and began to drag away the maiden who had been wearing a white dress but who now wore one of sky blue. They did not drag her off immediately, but sang with her for a long time before dragging her away. Three times they struck on something metallic behind the side scenes, and everyone got down on his knees and began to chant a prayer. Several times all of this activity was interrupted by enthusiastic shouts from the spectators.

The third act is described:

> . . . But suddenly a storm blew up. Chromatic scales and chords of diminished sevenths were heard in the orchestra. Everyone ran about and again they dragged one of the bystanders behind the scenes as the curtain fell.

In the fourth act, "There was some sort of devil who sang, waving

his hands, until the boards were moved out from under him and he
dropped down."[26]

In *Resurrection* Tolstoy describes the city and the court in the same
way; he uses a similar technique in "Kreutzer Sonata" when he
describes marriage—"Why, if people have an affinity of souls, must
they sleep together?" But he did not defamiliarize only those things
he sneered at:

> Pierre stood up from his new comrades and made his way between
> the campfires to the other side of the road where, it seemed, the captive
> soldiers were held. He wanted to talk with them. The French sentry
> stopped him on the road and ordered him to return. Pierre did so, but
> not to the campfire, not to his comrades, but to an abandoned, un-
> harnessed carriage. On the ground, near the wheel of the carriage, he
> sat cross-legged in the Turkish fashion, and lowered his head. He sat
> motionless for a long time, thinking. More than an hour passed. No one
> disturbed him. Suddenly he burst out laughing with his robust, good
> natured laugh—so loudly that the men near him looked around,
> surprised at his conspicuously strange laughter.
>
> "Ha, ha, ha," laughed Pierre. And he began to talk to himself. "The
> soldier didn't allow me to pass. They caught me, barred me. Me—me—
> my immortal soul. Ha, ha, ha," he laughed with tears starting in his
> eyes.
>
> Pierre glanced at the sky, into the depths of the departing, playing
> stars. "And all this is mine, all this is in me, and all this is I," thought
> Pierre. "And all this they caught and put in a planked enclosure."
> He smiled and went off to his comrades to lie down to sleep.[27]

Anyone who knows Tolstoy can find several hundred such passages
in his work. His method of seeing things out of their normal context
is also apparent in his last works. Tolstoy described the dogmas and
rituals he attacked as if they were unfamiliar, substituting everyday
meanings for the customarily religious meanings of the words
common in church ritual. Many persons were painfully wounded;
they considered it blasphemy to present as strange and monstrous
what they accepted as sacred. Their reaction was due chiefly to the

26. The Tolstoy and Gogol translations are ours. The passage occurs in Vol. II,
Part 8, Chap. 9 of the edition of *War and Peace* published in Boston by the Dana
Estes Co. in 1904–1912. *Ed. note.*

27. Leo Tolstoy, *War and Peace*, IV, Part 13. Chap. 14. *Ed. note.*

technique through which Tolstoy perceived and reported his environment. And after turning to what he had long avoided, Tolstoy found that his perceptions had unsettled his faith.

The technique of defamiliarization is not Tolstoy's alone. I cited Tolstoy because his work is generally known.

Now, having explained the nature of this technique, let us try to determine the approximate limits of its application. I personally feel that defamiliarization is found almost everywhere form is found. In other words, the difference between Potebnya's point of view and ours is this: An image is not a permanent referent for those mutable complexities of life which are revealed through it; its purpose is not to make us perceive meaning, but to create a special perception of the object—*it creates a "vision" of the object instead of serving as a means for knowing it.*

The purpose of imagery in erotic art can be studied even more accurately; an erotic object is usually presented as if it were seen for the first time. Gogol, in "Christmas Eve," provides the following example:

> Here he approached her more closely, coughed, smiled at her, touched her plump, bare arm with his fingers, and expressed himself in a way that showed both his cunning and his conceit.
>
> "And what is this you have, magnificent Solokha?" and having said this, he jumped back a little.
>
> "What? An arm, Osip Nikiforovich!" she answered.
>
> "Hmm, an arm! *He, he, he!*" said the secretary cordially, satisfied with his beginning. He wandered about the room.
>
> "And what is this you have, dearest Solokha?" he said in the same way, having approached her again and grasped her lightly by the neck, and in the very same way he jumped back.
>
> "As if you don't see, Osip Nikiforovich!" answered Solokha, "a neck, and on my neck a necklace."
>
> "Hmm! On the neck a necklace! *He, he, he!*" and the secretary again wandered about the room, rubbing his hands.
>
> "And what is this you have, incomparable Solokha?" . . . It is not known to what the secretary would stretch his long fingers now.

And Knut Hamsun has the following in "Hunger": "Two white prodigies appeared from beneath her blouse."

Erotic subjects may also be presented figuratively with the obvious purpose of leading us away from their "recognition." Hence sexual organs are referred to in terms of lock and key, [28] or quilting tools, [29] or bow and arrow, or rings and marlinspikes, as in the legend of Stavyor, in which a married man does not recognize his wife, who is disguised as a warrior. She proposes a riddle:

> "Remember, Stavyor, do you recall
> How we little ones walked to and fro in the street?
> You and I together sometimes played with a marlinspike—
> You had a silver marlinspike,
> But I had a gilded ring?
> I found myself at it just now and then,
> But you fell in with it ever and always."
> Says Stavyor, son of Godinovich,
> "What! I didn't play with you at marlinspikes!"
> Then Vasilisa Mikulichna: "So he says.
> Do you remember, Stavyor, do you recall,
> Now must you know, you and I together learned to
>   read and write;
> Mine was an ink-well of silver,
> And yours a pen of gold?
> But I just moistened it a little now and then,
> And I just moistened it ever and always." [30]

In a different version of the legend we find a key to the riddle:

> Here the formidable envoy Vasilyushka
> Raised her skirts to the very navel,
> And then the young Stavyor, son of Godinovich,
> Recognized her gilded ring . . . . [31]

But defamiliarization is not only a technique of the erotic riddle— a technique of euphemism—it is also the basis and point of all riddles. Every riddle pretends to show its subject either by words

28. [Dimitry] Savodnikov, *Zagadki russkovo naroda* [*Riddles of the Russian People*] (St. Petersburg, 1901), Nos. 102–107.

29. *Ibid.*, Nos. 588–591.

30. A. E. Gruzinsky, ed., *Pesni, sobrannye P[avel] N. Rybnikovym* [*Songs Collected by P. N. Rybnikov*] (Moscow, 1909–1910), No. 30.

31. *Ibid.*, No. 171.

which specify or describe it but which, during the telling, do not seem applicable (the type: "black and white and 'red'—read—all over) or by means of odd but imitative sounds ("'Twas brillig, and the slithy toves/Did gyre and gimble in the wabe").[32]

Even erotic images not intended as riddles are defamiliarized ("boobies," "tarts," "piece," etc.). In popular imagery there is generally something equivalent to "trampling the grass" and "breaking the guelder-rose." The technique of defamiliarization is absolutely clear in the widespread image—a motif of erotic affectation—in which a bear and other wild beasts (or a devil, with a different reason for nonrecognition) do not recognize a man.[33]

The lack of recognition in the following tale is quite typical:

> A peasant was plowing a field with a piebald mare. A bear approached him and asked, "Uncle, what's made this mare piebald for you?"
>
> "I did the piebalding myself."
>
> "But how?"
>
> "Let me, and I'll do the same for you."
>
> The bear agreed. The peasant tied his feet together with a rope, took the ploughshare from the two-wheeled plough, heated it on the fire, and applied it to his flanks. He made the bear piebald by scorching his fur down to the hide with the hot ploughshare. The man untied the bear, which went off and lay down under a tree.
>
> A magpie flew at the peasant to pick at the meat on his shirt. He caught her and broke one of her legs. The magpie flew off to perch in the same tree under which the bear was lying. Then, after the magpie, a horsefly landed on the mare, sat down, and began to bite. The peasant caught the fly, took a stick, shoved it up its rear, and let it go. The fly

32. We have supplied familiar English examples in place of Shklovsky's wordplay. Shklovsky is saying that we create words with no referents or with ambiguous referents in order to force attention to the objects represented by the similar-sounding words. By making the reader go through the extra step of interpreting the nonsense word, the writer prevents an automatic response. A toad is a toad, but "tove" forces one to pause and think about the beast. *Ed. note.*

33. E. R. Romanov, "Besstrashny barin," *Velikorusskiye skazki* (Zapiski Imperskovo Russkovo Geograf007cheskovo Obschestva, XLII, No. 52). Belorussky sbornik, "Spravyadlivy soldat" ["The Intrepid Gentleman," *Great Russian Tales* (Notes of the Imperial Russian Geographical Society, XLII, No. 52). White Russian Anthology, "The Upright Soldier" (1886–1912)].

went to the tree where the bear and the magpie were. There all three sat.

The peasant's wife came to bring his dinner to the field. The man and his wife finished their dinner in the fresh air, and he began to wrestle with her on the ground.

The bear saw this and said to the magpie and the fly, "Holy priests! The peasant wants to piebald someone again."

The magpie said, "No, he wants to break someone's legs."

The fly said, "No, he wants to shove a stick up someone's rump." [34]

The similarity of technique here and in Tolstoy's "Kholstomer," is, I think, obvious.

Quite often in literature the sexual act itself is defamiliarized; for example, the *Decameron* refers to "scraping out a barrel," "catching nightingales," "gay wool-beating work," (the last is not developed in the plot). Defamiliarization is often used in describing the sexual organs.

A whole series of plots is based on such a lack of recognition; for example, in Afanasyev's *Intimate Tales* the entire story of "The Shy Mistress" is based on the fact that an object is not called by its proper name—or, in other words, on a game of nonrecognition. So too in Onchukov's "Spotted Petticoats," tale no. 525, and also in "The Bear and the Hare" from *Intimate Tales*, in which the bear and the hare make a "wound."

Such constructions as "the pestle and the mortar," or "Old Nick and the infernal regions" (*Decameron*), are also examples of the technique of defamiliarization. And in my article on plot construction I write about defamiliarization in psychological parallelism. Here, then, I repeat that the perception of disharmony in a harmonious context is important in parallelism. The purpose of parallelism, like the general purpose of imagery, is to transfer the usual perception of an object into the sphere of a new perception—that is, to make a unique semantic modification.

In studying poetic speech in its phonetic and lexical structure as well as in its characteristic distribution of words and in the characteristic thought structures compounded from the words, we find

34. D[mitry] S. Zelenin, *Velikorusskiye skazki Permskoy gubernii* [*Great Russian Tales of the Permian Province* (St. Petersburg, 1913)], No. 70.

everywhere the artistic trademark—that is, we find material obviously created to remove the automatism of perception; the author's purpose is to create the vision which results from that deautomatized perception. A work is created "artistically" so that its perception is impeded and the greatest possible effect is produced through the slowness of the perception. As a result of this lingering, the object is perceived not in its extension in space, but, so to speak, in its continuity. Thus "poetic language" gives satisfaction. According to Aristotle, poetic language must appear strange and wonderful; and, in fact, it is often actually foreign: the Sumerian used by the Assyrians, the Latin of Europe during the Middle Ages, the Arabisms of the Persians, the Old Bulgarian of Russian literature, or the elevated, almost literary language of folk songs. The common archaisms of poetic language, the intricacy of the sweet new style [dolce stil nuovo],[35] the obscure style of the language of Arnaut Daniel with the "roughened" [harte] forms which make pronunciation difficult—these are used in much the same way. Leo Jakubinsky has demonstrated the principle of phonetic "roughening" of poetic language in the particular case of the repetition of identical sounds. The language of poetry is, then, a difficult, roughened, impeded language. In a few special instances the language of poetry approximates the language of prose, but this does not violate the principle of "roughened" form.

> Her sister was called Tatyana.
> For the first time we shall
> Wilfully brighten the delicate
> Pages of a novel with such a name.

wrote Pushkin. The usual poetic language for Pushkin's contemporaries was the elegant style of Derzhavin; but Pushkin's style, because it seemed trivial then, was unexpectedly difficult for them. We should remember the consternation of Pushkin's contemporaries over the vulgarity of his expressions. He used the popular language as a special device for prolonging attention, just as his contemporaries generally used Russian words in their usually French speech (see Tolstoy's examples in *War and Peace*).

35. Dante, *Purgatorio*, 24:56. Dante refers to the new lyric style of his contemporaries. *Ed. note.*

Just now a still more characteristic phenomenon is under way. Russian literary language, which was originally foreign to Russia, has so permeated the language of the people that it has blended with their conversation. On the other hand, literature has now begun to show a tendency towards the use of dialects (Remizov, Klyuyev, Essenin, and others,[36] so unequal in talent and so alike in language, are intentionally provincial) and of barbarisms (which gave rise to the Severyanin group[37]). And currently Maxim Gorky is changing his diction from the old literary language to the new literary colloquialism of Leskov.[38] Ordinary speech and literary language have thereby changed places (see the work of Vyacheslav Ivanov and many others). And finally, a strong tendency, led by Khlebnikov, to create a new and properly poetic language has emerged. In the light of these developments we can define poetry as *attenuated, tortuous* speech. Poetic speech is *formed speech*. Prose is ordinary speech— economical, easy, proper, the goddess of prose [*dea prosae*] is a goddess of the accurate, facile type, of the "direct" expression of a child. I shall discuss roughened form and retardation as the general *law* of art at greater length in an article on plot construction.[39]

Nevertheless, the position of those who urge the idea of the economy of artistic energy as something which exists in and even distinguishes poetic language seems, at first glance, tenable for the problem of rhythm. Spencer's description of rhythm would seem to be absolutely incontestable:

> Just as the body in receiving a series of varying concussions, must keep the muscles ready to meet the most violent of them, as not knowing when such may come: so, the mind in receiving unarranged articulations, must keep its perspectives active enough to recognize the least

36. Alexy Remizov (1877–1957) is best known as a novelist and satirist; Nicholas Klyuyev (1885–1937) and Sergey Essenin (1895–1925) were "peasant poets." All three were noted for their faithful reproduction of Russian dialects and colloquial language. *Ed. note.*

37. A group noted for its opulent and sensuous verse style. *Ed. note.*

38. Nicholas Leskov (1831–1895), novelist and short story writer, helped popularize the *skaz*, or yarn, and hence, because of the part dialect peculiarities play in the *skaz*, also altered Russian literary language. *Ed. note.*

39. Shklovsky is probably referring to his *Razvyortyvaniye syuzheta* [*Plot Development*] (Petrograd, 1921). *Ed. note.*

easily caught sounds. And as, if the concussions recur in definite order, the body may husband its forces by adjusting the resistance needful for each concussion; so, if the syllables be rhythmically arranged, the mind may economize its energies by anticipating the attention required for each syllable.[40]

This apparently conclusive observation suffers from the common fallacy, the confusion of the laws of poetic and prosaic language. In *The Philosophy of Style* Spencer failed utterly to distinguish between them. But rhythm may have two functions. The rhythm of prose, or of a work song like "Dubinushka," permits the members of the work crew to do their necessary "groaning together" and also eases the work by making it automatic. And, in fact, it is easier to march with music than without it, and to march during an animated conversation is even easier, for the walking is done unconsciously. Thus the rhythm of prose is an important automatizing element; the rhythm of poetry is not. There is "order" in art, yet not a single column of a Greek temple stands exactly in its proper order; poetic rhythm is similarly disordered rhythm. Attempts to systematize the irregularities have been made, and such attempts are part of the current problem in the theory of rhythm. It is obvious that the systematization will not work, for in reality the problem is not one of complicating the rhythm but of disordering the rhythm—a disordering which cannot be predicted. Should the disordering of rhythm become a convention, it would be ineffective as a device for the roughening of language. But I will not discuss rhythm in more detail since I intend to write a book about it.[41]

Victor Shklovsky, "Iskusstvo, kak priyom," *Sborniki*, II (1917).

40. Spencer, [p. 169. Again the Russian text is shortened from Spencer's original].

41. We have been unable to discover the book Shklovsky promised. *Ed. note.*

Sterne's *Tristram Shandy*:
Stylistic Commentary

To a certain extent, Shklovsky's essay on Tristram Shandy [1] *is an application of the principles stated in "Art as Technique," but with material added by the development of the Formalist methodology between 1917 and 1921. Shklovsky's basic assumption, announced in the earlier essay, is that the business of literary criticism is to discuss the literariness of literature, to discuss that which makes literature different from other kinds of discourse. In the case of the novel, this quickly led the Formalists to distinguish between story and plot. Although Tomashevsky's "Thematics" (see pp. 66–78) shows the distinction clearly, a few words about it are in order here.*

Story is essentially the temporal-causal sequence of narrated events. Its formula, capable of infinite extension, is always "because of A, then B." Because Raskolnikov is an impoverished intellectual, he killed . . . ; because Pip fed a convict, ... Such is the pattern of the story, each event coming in the order in which it would occur in real life and the events bound each to each in a cause-and-effect relationship. This, to return to the notion of defamiliarization, is the familiar way of telling something; but precisely because it is the familiar way, it is not the artistic way. Artistry, for Shklovsky, requires both defamiliarization and an obvious display of the devices by which the familiar is made strange.

In these terms, plot becomes the story as distorted or defamiliarized in the process of telling. Even a novel as superficially simple in construction as Hawthorne's The Scarlet Letter *distorts both temporal and cause-effect relations by, for example, beginning in the middle, after the adultery that properly begins the main action. Or such a seemingly orthodox novel as*

1. The title of the monograph is Tristram Shandy *Sterna i teoriya romana* [*Sterne's* Tristram Shandy *and the Theory of the Novel*] (Petrograd, 1921). The title given on the first page of the text is Tristram Shandy *Sterna: Stilistichesky kommentary*, the title we have used. The monograph was reprinted in Shklovsky's *O teorii prozy* [*On the Theory of Prose*] (Moscow, 1925 and 1929). We have used the 1921 text.

Vanity Fair *has plot rather than story partly by virtue of the parallel development of two strands that are causally unrelated—the Becky Sharp strand and the Amelia Sedley strand. As Shklovsky shows in his study of* Tristram Shandy, *the ways of making a story into a plot are innumerable, but all involve some kind of disarrangement of what we could call the natural, or real-life, sequence of events. Since plot distinguishes the natural from the artistic method of narration, Shklovsky is interested in plot.*[2]

*As a result, Shklovsky can logically conclude his essay with the apparent exaggeration that "*Tristram Shandy *is the most typical novel in world literature." What he means is that it is the most plotted, the least "storied," of any major novel. Cause and effect in the ordinary sense hardly exist in* Shandy's *world.*[3] *Moreover, the techniques by which Sterne makes a plot from* Shandy's *story are not realistically "motivated."*[4] *As Tomashevsky will explain later, "motivation" is the reason for the use of a device, word, or any element that gets into a literary work.*

In the conventional novel, so the theory runs, a number of the included elements may be accounted for as attempts to achieve verisimilitude (Hawthorne's elaborate description of how he found the scarlet letter; Hester's beauty and passionate nature and Chillingworth's age and coldness, which make the adultery of an otherwise noble woman seem plausible, etc.). When Shklovsky says that a technique is "unmotivated," he means simply that we cannot provide a satisfactory realistic reason for its presence. A device so used is "revealed," or "displayed," or "laid bare"; it exists more to be noticed by the reader than to function in the work. But as Shklovsky recognizes, the distinction is not always clear-cut. The digressions on "noseology," for example, help account for Shandy's character, but they are also "revealed" because Sterne is at great pains to make the reader aware that they are digressions. Generally, if we are more aware of the technique than of its function, it is "revealed" or "laid bare."

Although the implication that a novel exists merely to display the technique of its author seems like the most blatant aestheticism, it must be remembered

2. See also Tomashevsky's "Thematics," below, pp. 66–67.

3. This is only partly true—or, we should say, only literally true. In a sense, cause and effect is the theme of *Tristram Shandy*, but Sterne is interested in the psychological cause and effect of the association of ideas rather than in physical cause and effect.

4. See below, pp. 80–84.

that in "Art as Technique" Shklovsky argued that only through artistry are our perceptions sharpened.[5] Because we keep stumbling over the literary devices in Tristram Shandy, *Shklovsky could consistently have argued, we must attend to them and through them to the universe that Sterne has created.*

In this essay I do not propose to analyze Laurence Sterne's novel, but rather to illustrate general laws of plot. Formalistically, Sterne was an extreme revolutionary; it was characteristic of him to "lay bare" his technique. The artistic form is presented simply as such, without any kind of motivation. The difference between a novel by Sterne and the ordinary kind of novel is exactly that between ordinary poetry with its phonetic instrumentation and the poetry of the Futurists, written in obscure language.[6] Yet nothing much is written about Sterne any more; or, if it is, it consists only of a few banalities.

The first impression upon taking up Sterne's *Tristram Shandy* and beginning to read it is one of chaos. The action is continually interrupted; the author repeatedly goes backward or leaps forward; whole ten-page passages are filled with whimsical discussions about fortifications or about the influence of a person's nose or name on his character. Such digressions are unrelated to the basic narrative.

Although the beginning of the book has the tone of an autobiography, it drifts into a description of the hero's ancestors. In fact, the hero's birth is long delayed by the irrelevant material squeezed into the novel. The description of a single day takes up much of the book; I quote Sterne himself:

> I will not finish that sentence till I have made an observation upon the strange state of affairs between the reader and myself, just as things stand at present—an observation never applicable before to any one biographical writer since the creation of the world, but to myself—and I believe will never hold good to any other, until its final destruction—

5. See above, p. 12.
6. That is, in ordinary poetry the "phonetic instrumentation"—rhyme, meter, alliteration, etc.—is often said to accompany a "meaning," to which it is subordinate; Futurist poetry called attention to, or "laid bare," the devices of instrumentation. *Tristram Shandy* is like Futurist poetry in that it also calls attention to technical devices that are usually subordinated. *Ed. note.*

and therefore, for the very novelty of it alone, it must be worth your worships attending to.

I am this month one whole year older than I was this time twelve-month; and having got, as you perceive, almost into the middle of my fourth volume—and no farther than to my first day's life—'tis demonstrative that I have three hundred and sixty-four days more life to write just now, than when I first set out; so that instead of advancing, as a common writer, in my work with what I have been doing at it—on the contrary, I am just thrown so many volumes back—[pp. 285–286].[7]

But when you begin to examine the structure of the book, you see first of all that the disorder is intentional and, in this case, poetic. It is strictly regulated, like a picture by Picasso. Everything in the book is displaced; everything is transposed. The dedication occurs on page 15, contrary to the three basic requirements of content, form, and place. Nor is the Preface in its usual position. It takes up approximately a quire, not at the beginning of the book but rather in Volume III, Chapter 20, pages 192 through 203. Sterne justifies the Preface in this way: "All my heroes are off my hands;—'tis the first time I have had a moment to spare,—and I'll make use of it, and write my preface" (p. 192). The Preface contains, of course, as many entanglements as ingenuity permits. But the most radical of the displacements is the transposition of entire chapters (Chapters 18 and 19 of Volume IX are placed after Chapter 25). Sterne justifies the transposition so: "All I wish is, that it may be a lesson to the world, *to let people tell their stories their own way*" (p. 633).

But this transposition of chapters reveals another of Sterne's basic techniques—that of impeding the flow of the action. In the beginning, Sterne introduces an anecdote about an act of sexual intercourse interrupted by a woman's question (p. 5). Here is how the anecdote is brought in. Tristram Shandy's mother sleeps with his father only on the first Sunday of each month and on precisely that evening Mr. Shandy winds the clock in order to get both of these domestic duties "out of the way at one time, and be no more plagued and

7. Shklovsky read the Russian version of *Tristram Shandy* published in the journal *Panteon Literatury* [*Pantheon of Literature*] in 1892. Our quotations are taken from *The Life and Opinions of Tristram Shandy, Gentleman*, ed. James Aiken Work (New York: Odyssey Press, 1940); all page and chapter references are to this edition. *Ed. note.*

pester'd with them the rest of the month" (p. 8). As a result, an unavoidable association has formed in his wife's mind, so that she "could never hear the said clock wound up,—but the thoughts of some other things unavoidably popp'd into her head,—& *vice versa*" (p. 9). Here is the exact question with which Tristram's mother interrupted the activity of his father: "*Pray, my dear, . . . have you not forgot to wind up the clock?*" (p. 5).

This anecdote is introduced into the work first by a general comment upon the inattentiveness of the parents (pp. 4–5), then by the mother's question, the context of which we do not yet know. At first we think she had merely interrupted the father's conversation. Sterne plays with our error:

> *Good G——!* cried my father, making an exclamation, but taking care to moderate his voice at the same time,—*Did ever woman, since the creation of the world, interrupt a man with such a silly question?* Pray, what was your father saying?—Nothing [p. 5].

Then his remarks about the homunculus (fetus) are spiced with anecdotal references to its right to legal defense (pp. 5–6). Only on pages 8 through 9 do we get an explanation of this whole passage and a description of the odd punctiliousness of the father in his family affairs.

Thus, from the very beginning, we find displacement of time in *Tristram Shandy*. The causes follow the consequences, and the author himself prepares the groundwork for erroneous assumptions. This is one of Sterne's characteristic techniques. The quibbling about the coitus motif itself, related to a definite day and referring back to what has already happened in the novel, reappears from time to time and ties together the various sections of this masterfully constructed and unusually complicated work.

If we visualize the digressions schematically, they will appear as cones representing an event, with the apex representing the causes. In an ordinary novel such a cone is joined to the main story line at its apex; in *Tristram Shandy* the base of the cone is joined to the main story line, so that all at once we fall into a swarm of allusions.

As we know, this same technique occurs in one of Andrey Bely's last novels, *Kotik Latayev*; it is motivated by the fact that the novel shows the formation of a world from chaos. Out of the swarming mass appears an established order, with layers of puns on the names of the substances in the order stratifying and giving form to the mass.

Such time shifts occur often enough in the poetics of the novel. Consider, for example, the time shift in [Turgenev's] *A Nest of Gentlefolk* (the shift is motivated by Lavertsky's reminiscence) or in [Goncharov's] "The Dream of Oblomov."[8] In Gogol's *Dead Souls* no reasons are given for the time shifts (back to Chichikov's childhood and Tentetnikov's upbringing). Sterne, however, spread the technique throughout the entire work.

Exposition, preparation for a new character, always occurs after we have paused in perplexity over a strange word or an exclamation from that character. Here we have the exposure of the technique. In *Tales of Belkin*—in "The Shot," for example—Pushkin made extensive use of time shifts. In "The Shot" we first see Silvio practicing his marksmanship; next we hear Silvio's story about the unfinished duel; then we meet the Count, Silvio's enemy, and learn the outcome of the story. The parts are in a II–I–III order, and we see a reason for the shift; Sterne, however, simply lays bare the technique.

As I have said already, Sterne thought such [aesthetic] motivation an end in itself.[9] He wrote:

> What I have to inform you, comes, I own, a little out of its due course;—for it should have been told a hundred and fifty pages ago, but that I foresaw then 'twould come in pat hereafter, and be of more advantage here than elsewhere [p. 144].

Sterne even lays bare the technique of combining separate story lines to make up the novel. In general, he accentuates the very structure of the novel. By violating the form, he forces us to attend to it; and,

8. A section of Goncharov's novel *Oblomov* (Part I, Chap. 9), originally published separately. *Ed. note.*

9. "Motivation" as used by the Formalists is a complex concept. Generally, motivation is the reason governing the use of a particular device and may include everything from the author's desire to shock his readers, to the necessity of including specific props required by the action. See below, pp. 78–87. *Ed. note.*

for him, this awareness of the form through its violation constitutes the content of the novel.

In my little book on *Don Quixote*,[10] I have already noted several conventional methods of splicing story lines to form a novel. Sterne used still other methods or, using an old one, did not hide its conventionality but rather thrust it out protrudingly and toyed with it. In an ordinary novel digressions are cut off by a return to the main story. If there are two, or only a few, story lines in the novel, their fragments alternate with one another—as in *Don Quixote*, where the scenes showing the adventures of the knight in the court of the Duke alternate with scenes depicting the governorship of Sancho Panza. Zielinski notes something entirely different in Homer. Homer never shows two simultaneous actions. If by force of circumstances they ever had to be simultaneous, they were reported as happening in sequence. Only the activity of one character and the "standing pat" (that is, the inactivity) of another can occur simultaneously. Sterne allowed actions to occur simultaneously, and he even parodied the development of the story line and the instrusions of the new material into it.

The description of Tristram Shandy's birth is the subject of the story line developed in the first part. The topic covers 203 pages, which nevertheless contain almost nothing about the actual birth of Tristram Shandy. For the most part, they deal with the conversation between the hero's father and his uncle Toby. Here is how the development takes place:

—I wonder what's all i··at noise, and running backwards and forwards for, above stairs, quoth my father, addressing himself, after an hour and a half's silence, to my uncle *Toby*,—who you must know, was sitting on the opposite side of the fire, smoking his social pipe all the time, in mute contemplation of a new pair of black-plush-breeches which he had got on;—What can they be doing brother? quoth my father,—we can scarce hear ourselves talk.

I think, replied my uncle *Toby*, taking his pipe from his mouth, and striking the head of it two or three times upon the nail of his left thumb,

10. Victor Shklovsky, *Kak sledan* Don Quixote [*How* Don Quixote *Was Made*], reprinted in *O teorii prozy. Ed. note.*

as he began his sentence,—I think, says he:—But to enter rightly into
my uncle *Toby's* sentiments upon this matter, you must be made to
enter first a little into his character, the out-lines of which I shall just
give you, and then the dialogue between him and my father will go on
as well again [p. 63].

Then begins a discussion of inconstancy so whimsical that it would
have to be quoted to be communicated properly. On page 65 Sterne
remembers, "But I forget my uncle *Toby*, whom all this while we
have left knocking the ashes out of his tobacco pipe." Then begins a
sketch of Uncle Toby into which the story of Aunt Dinah is inserted.
On page 72, Sterne remembers: "I was just going, for example, to
have given you the great out-lines of my uncle *Toby's* most whimsical
character;—when my aunt *Dinah* and the coachman came a-cross
us, and led us a vagary . . . ." Unfortunately, I cannot include
everything Sterne has written, so I shall continue with a large
omission:

> from the beginning of this, you see, I have constructed the main work
> and the adventitious parts of it with such intersections, and have so
> complicated and involved the digressive and progressive movements,
> one wheel within another, that the whole machine, in general, has been
> kept a-going;—and, what's more, it shall be kept a-going these forty
> years, if it pleases the fountain of health to bless me so long with life
> and good spirits [pp. 73–74].

So ends Chapter 22; Chapter 23 continues: "I have a strong
propensity in me to begin this chapter very nonsensically, and I will
not balk my fancy.—Accordingly I set off thus." And new digressions
are in store for us. On page 77 there is a further reminder: "If I was
not morally sure that the reader must be out of all patience for my
uncle *Toby's* character, . . ." and further down the page we find a
description of Uncle Toby's "Hobby-Horse," his mania. It seems
that Uncle Toby, wounded in the groin at the siege of Namur, was
drawn into the erection of toy fortifications. Finally, on page 99,
Uncle Toby can finish the activity he began on page 63:

> I think, replied my uncle *Toby*,—taking, as I told you, his pipe from
> his mouth, and striking the ashes out of it as he began his sentence;—I
> think, replied he,—it would not be amiss, brother, if we rung the bell.

Sterne repeatedly resorts to this technique; and, as we see from his facetious reminders about Uncle Toby, not only is he fully aware of the exaggerations in his use of it, but he even enjoys playing around with it.

This manner of development, as I have already noted, is the characteristic pattern of Sterne's work. For example, on page 144, uncle Toby says, "I wish, . . . you had seen what prodigious armies we had in *Flanders*." Further on, the material about the mania of Tristram's father begins to develop. In fact, Tristram's father has attached to himself the following manias: on the harmful influence of the pressure brought to bear on the head of an infant when a woman experiences labor pains (pp. 149–154), on the influence of a man's name upon his character (a motif developed in great detail), and on the influence of the size of a man's nose on his potential greatness (this motif is developed in an unusually ostentatious way, approximately from page 217, when, after a short break, curious stories about noseology begin to develop). The Tale of Slawkenbergius is especially remarkable; Tristram's father knows ten decades of ten tales each, all with stories about Slawkenbergius. The development of the noseology ends on page 272.

Mr. Shandy's other manias also play a part in this particular development—that is, Sterne sidetracks our attention to talk about them.

The main story resumes on page 157:

—"*I wish*, Dr. *Slop*," quoth my uncle *Toby* (repeating his wish for Dr. *Slop* a second time, and with a degree of more zeal and earnestness in his manner of wishing, than he had wished it at first)—"*I wish*, Dr. *Slop*," quoth my uncle *Toby*, "*you had seen what prodigious armies we had in Flanders.*"

Once again the expansion of the material interrupts. And on page 163: "What prodigious armies you had in *Flanders*!" In Sterne, conscious exaggeration of the expansion frequently occurs without the use of a transitional sentence.

The moment my father got up into his chamber, he threw himself prostrate across his bed in the wildest disorder imaginable, but at the same time, in the most lamentable attitude of a man borne down with sorrows, that ever the eye of pity dropp'd a tear for [pp. 215–216].

An exact description of his posture follows; such descriptions are very characteristic of Sterne:

> The palm of his right hand, as he fell upon the bed, receiving his fore-head, and covering the greatest part of both his eyes, gently sunk down with his head (his elbow giving way backwards) till his nose touch'd the quilt;—his left arm hung insensible over the side of the bed, his knuckles reclining upon the handle of the chamber pot, which peep'd out beyond the valance,—his right leg (his left being drawn up towards his body) hung half over the side of the bed, the edge of it pressing upon his shin-bone.

Mr. Shandy's despondency is brought on by the fact that the bridge of his son's nose had been crushed by the obstetrical tongs during delivery and, as I have already said, an entire literary cycle on noses follows. On page 273 we finally return to the man we left lying on the bed:

> My father lay stretched across the bed as still as if the hand of death had pushed him down, for a full hour and a half, before he began to play upon the floor with the toe of that foot which hung over the bed-side.

I cannot help saying a few words in general about the postures we find in Sterne. The first to introduce the description of postures into the novel, he always portrayed them strangely—or, more exactly, he defamiliarized them. I shall cite an example: "Brother *Toby*, replied my father, taking his wig from off his head with his right hand, and with his *left* pulling a striped *India* handkerchief from his right coat pocket, . . ." (p. 158). I go directly to page 159:

> It was not an easy matter in any king's reign, (unless you were as lean a subject as myself) to have forced your hand diagonally, quite across your whole body, so as to gain the bottom of your opposite coat-pocket.

The method of portraying postures passed from Sterne to Leo Tolstoy,[11] who used it more flexibly and with psychological motivation.

11. Shklovsky here has a one-word parenthetical insertion "Eichenbaum," perhaps indicating that he saw Eichenbaum's *Molodoy Tolstoy* [*Young Tolstoy*] (Petrograd and Berlin, 1922), before its publication. *Ed. note.*

I now return to Sterne's technique of plot development with several examples which clearly establish the fact that awareness of form constitutes the subject matter of the novel.

> What a chapter of chances, said my father, turning himself about upon the first landing, as he and my uncle *Toby* were going down stairs —what a long chapter of chances do the events of this world lay open to us! [p. 279].

(Then follows a discussion containing an erotic element which I shall say more about later.)

> Is it not a shame to make two chapters of what passed in going down one pair of stairs? for we are got no farther yet than to the first landing, and there are fifteen more steps down to the bottom; and for aught I know, as my father and my uncle *Toby* are in a talking humour, there may be as many chapters as steps [p. 281].

Sterne devotes all of this chapter to a discussion of chapters.

The next chapter begins: "We shall bring all things to rights, said my father, setting his foot upon the first step from the landing—" (p. 283). And the next: "And how does your mistress? cried my father, taking the same step over again from the landing, . . ." (p. 284). And the next:

> Holla!—you chairman!—here's sixpence—do step into that bookseller's shop, and call me a *day-tall* critick. I am very willing to give any one of 'em a crown to help me with his tackling, to get my father and my uncle *Toby* off the stairs, and to put them to bed. . . .
>
> I am this month one whole year older than I was this time twelvemonth; and having got, as you perceive, almost into the middle of my fourth volume—and no farther than to my first day's life—'tis demonstrative that I have three hundred and sixty-four days more to write just now, than when I first set out; so that instead of advancing, as a common writer, in my work with what I have been doing at it—on the contrary, I am just thrown so many volumes back—[pp. 285–286].

The conventionality of this organization of the form is reminiscent of those octaves and sonnets filled with the description of how they were composed.

Here is one last example of such expansion in Sterne:

> My mother was going very gingerly in the dark along the passage which led to the parlour, as my uncle *Toby* pronounced the word *wife.*—

'Tis a shrill, penetrating sound of itself, and *Obadiah* had helped it by leaving the door a little a-jar, so that my mother heard enough of it, to imagine herself the subject of the conversation: so laying the edge of her finger across her two lips—holding in her breath, and bending her head a little downwards, with a twist of her neck—(not towards the door, but from it, by which means her ear was brought to the chink)—she listened with all her powers:—the listening slave, with the Goddess of Silence at his back, could not have given a finer thought for an intaglio.

In this attitude I am determined to let her stand for five minutes: till I bring up the affairs of the kitchen (as *Rapin* does those of the church) to the same period [pp. 357–358].

And on page 367: "I am a *Turk* if I had not as much forgot my mother, as if Nature had plaistered me up, and set me down naked upon the banks of the river Nile, ..." But there is another digression even after this reminder. The reminder is necessary merely to renew our awareness of the "forgotten mother" in order to prevent the impression of the expansion from fading.

At last, on page 370, the mother shifts her position: "Then, cried my mother, opening the door, ..."

In this case Sterne expands the material by including a second parallel story; in such cases in novels, ordinary time is usually thought to be suspended, or at least not considered, as opposed to showing the passage of time by explicit appeals to our reason. Shakespeare used his interpolated scenes to suspend time—that is, to divert attention from the normal flow of time; and even if the entire inserted dialogue (invariably with new characters) continued only a few minutes, Shakespeare felt it permissible to carry on the action as if hours or even a whole night had gone by. (We assume that curtains were not lowered, for it is very likely that curtains were not used in the Shakespearean theater because of the projecting stage.) Sterne, by repeatedly mentioning and reminding us of the fact that the mother has been standing in a stooped position for the whole time, forces us to notice his handling of it.

It is interesting, in a general way, to study the role time plays in Sterne's works. "Literary time" is clearly arbitrary; its laws do not coincide with the laws of ordinary time. If one studies, for example, the numerous tales and events concentrated in *Don Quixote*, he will see that the beginning of day and the beginning of night play no compositional role in the sequence of events—that, in general, the slow, lingering passage of the day does not exist. L'Abbé Prévost narrates *Manon Lescaut* in precisely the same way. Chevalier des Grieux tells the whole first part (seven folios) without a break; then, after a slight respite, continues for another seven folios. Such a conversation would have lasted sixteen hours, even under conditions allowing for rapid speech.

I have already spoken of the arbitrariness of time on the stage. But Sterne conceived of and used the arbitrariness of "literary time" as material for a game, as in Volume II, Chapter 8:

> It is about an hour and a half's tolerable good reading since my uncle *Toby* rung the bell, when *Obadiah* was order'd to saddle a horse, and go for Dr. *Slop* the man-midwife;—so that no one can say, with reason, that I have not allowed *Obadiah* time enough, poetically speaking, and considering the emergency too, both to go and come;—tho', morally and truly speaking, the man, perhaps, has scarce had time to get on his boots.
>
> If the hypercritic will go upon this; and is resolved after all to take a pendulum, and measure the true distance betwixt the ringing of the bell, and the rap at the door;—and, after finding it to be no more than two minutes, thirteen seconds, and three fifths,—should take upon him to insult over me for such a breach in unity, or rather probability, of time;—I would remind him, that the idea of duration and of its simple modes, is got merely from the train and succession of our ideas,—and is the true scholastic pendulum,—and by which, as a scholar, I will be tried in this matter,—adjuring and detesting the jurisdiction of all other pendulums whatever.
>
> I would, therefore, desire him to consider that it is but poor eight miles from *Shandy-Hall* to Dr. *Slop*, the man mid-wife's house;—and that whilst *Obadiah* has been going those said miles and back, I have brought my uncle *Toby* from *Namur*, quite across all *Flanders*, into *England*:—That I have had him ill upon my hands near four years;—and have since travelled him and Corporal *Trim*, in a chariot and four, a journey of near two hundred miles down into *Yorkshire*;—all which put together, must have prepared the reader's imagination for the entrance of Dr. *Slop* upon the stage, —as much, at least (I hope) as a dance, a song, or a concerto between the acts.
>
> If my hypercritic is intractable, alledging, that two minutes and

thirteen seconds are no more than two minutes and thirteen seconds,—
when I have said all I can about them;—and that this plea, tho' it might
save me dramatically, will damn me biographically, rendering my
book, from this very moment, a profess'd Romance, which, before was
a book aprocryphal:—If I am thus pressed—I then put an end to the
whole objection and controversy about it all at once,—by acquainting
him, that *Obadiah* had not got above three-score yards from the stable-
yard before he met with Dr. *Slop*; . . . [pp. 103–104].

Sterne took the device of the "discovered manuscript" almost
unchanged from among the old literary devices. Thus we find
Yorick's sermon in the novel. But, of course, the reading of this
discovered manuscript does not of itself represent a long digression
from the novel, for the sermon is repeatedly interrupted, chiefly by
emotional ejaculations. The course of the sermon occupies pages 125
through 140, but it is greatly expanded by insertions of the usual
Sternean kind.

The reading of the sermon begins with a description of Corporal
Trim's posture, depicted in Sterne's usual purposely awkward way:

> He stood before them with his body swayed, and bent forward just
> so far, as to make an angle of 85 degrees and a half upon the plain of
> the horizon;—which sound orators, to whom I address this, know very
> well, to be the true persuasive angle of incidence [p. 122].

And so it continues to:

> He stood,—for I repeat it, to take the picture of him in at one view,
> with his body sway'd, and somewhat bent forwards,—his right-leg firm
> under him, sustaining seven-eighths of his whole weight,—the foot of
> his left-leg, the defect of which was no disadvantage to his attitude,
> advanced a little,—not laterally, nor forwards, but in a line betwixt
> them; . . . .

And so on. The entire description continues for more than a page.
The sermon itself is interrupted by a story about Corporal Trim's
brother. Then come the theological protests of a Roman Catholic
(pp. 125, 126, 128, 129, etc.) and Uncle Toby's remarks on fortifications (pp. 133, 134, etc.) Thus while following the course of the
manuscript, Sterne also integrates it into the novel to a far greater
degree than does Cervantes.

Sterne made the "discovered manuscript" a favorite technique in his *Sentimental Journey*. He finds, as he sets out to do, a manuscript by Rabelais; but, as is quite typical of Sterne, he interrupts the manuscript with a discussion about wrapping merchandise. (Sterne has made the unfinished tale acceptable in both its motivated and unmotivated forms.) The interruption of the introduced manuscript is motivated by the fact that its conclusion has been lost. On the other hand, nothing motivates the conclusion of *Tristram Shandy*, which ends with a simple cutting off of the narrative:

> L—d! said my mother, what is all this story about?—
> A COCK and a BULL, said *Yorick*—and one of the best of its kind, I ever heard.
> The END of the NINTH VOLUME.

So also ends *Sentimental Journey*: "So that when I stretch'd out my hand, I caught hold of the Fille de Chambre's—" and it ends there.

This, of course, is a specific stylistic device based upon a variety of things. Sterne worked against a background of the adventure novel with its extraordinarily strict forms and with its formal rule to end with a wedding in the offing. In Sterne's novels the usual forms are changed and violated; it is not surprising that he handled the conclusions of his novels in the same way. We seem to stumble upon them, as if we found a trap door on a staircase where we had expected a landing. Gogol's "Ivan Fyodorovich Shponka and His Aunt"[12] is a short story concluded in the same way; but the conclusion is motivated, for the end of the manuscript was "lost" while baking pies (Sterne wraps currant jam in his). The notes comprising E. T. A. Hoffmann's *Kater Murr* depend upon the same technique, with the nonexistent conclusion motivated by complicated time shifts and parallelism (justified by the fact that the pages are not in order).

Sterne introduces the story of Le Fever in his usual way: During a conversation about the choice of a tutor for Tristram, at the time of Tristram's birth, Uncle Toby suggests the son of poor Le Fever,

12. From Nicholas Gogol's *Evenings on a Farm Near Dikanka. Ed. note.*

and the story immediately begins, narrated not by Toby but by Tristram Shandy himself:

> Then, brother *Shandy*, answered my uncle *Toby*, raising himself off the chair, and laying down his pipe to take hold of my father's other hand, —I humbly beg I may recommend poor *Le Fever's* son to you;—a tear of joy of the first water sparkled in my uncle *Toby's* eye,—and another, the fellow to it, in the corporal's, as the proposition was made;—you will see why when you read *Le Fever's* story:—fool that I was! nor can I recollect, (nor perhaps you) without turning back to the place, what it was that hindered me from letting the corporal tell it in his own words; —but the occasion is lost,—I must tell it now in my own [pp. 415–416].

The story about Le Fever, which runs from page 416 to page 432, then begins.

A separate cycle of stories (pp. 479–538) describes Tristram's travels. Sterne later developed this episode, step by step and motif by motif, into his *Sentimental Journey*. Sterne also inserts a story about the Abbess of Andoüillets into the account of Tristram's journey (pp. 504–510).

All of this diverse material, which is augmented by extensive excerpts from the works of various pedants, would undoubtedly tear the novel to bits were it not drawn together by crisscrossing motifs.[13] A stated motif is never fully developed, never actually realized, but is only recalled from time to time; its fulfillment is continually put off to a more and more remote time. Yet its very presence in all the dimensions of the novel ties the episodes together.

There are several such motifs, one of them concerning knots. Here is how it appears—Dr. Slop's bag of obstetrical instruments is tied up in several knots:

> 'Tis God's mercy, quoth he [Dr. Slop], (to himself) that Mrs. *Shandy* has had so bad a time of it,—else she might have been brought to bed seven times told, before one half of these knots could have got untied [p. 167].

13. This passage is interesting because it is one of the few in which Shklovsky shows his sense of the importance of unity in fiction. It can be said in Shklovsky's defense that he felt he had to take the novel apart before he could know how it worked. Moreover, he was usually interested either in a particular technique in itself or in showing departures from such norms as unity. *Ed. note.*

In the next chapter, same page:

> In the case of *knots*,—by which, in the first place, I would not be understood to mean slip-knots,—because in the course of my life and opinions,—my opinions concerning them will come in more properly when I mention . . . .

And so on. Then begins a discussion about knots, hitches, fastenings, bows, and so on endlessly. Meanwhile, Dr. Slop gets a little knife and cuts the knots, but accidentally wounds his hand. Then he begins to swear, but the elder Shandy "with Cervantes-like seriousness" suggests he not swear in vain, but rather curse in accordance with the rules of art and, in lieu of a handbook, hands him the formula of excommunication from the Roman Catholic church. Slop takes it and reads; the formula occupies two pages. The curious thing here is the motivation Sterne uses to develop the material. Usually such material has to do with medieval scholarship, which by Sterne's time was already considered laughable (just as, in stories about foreigners, it is thought funny when they pronounce words according to their own dialectical peculiarities). These medieval materials are usually introduced into the story merely as manias of Tristram's father. In this case, however, the motivation is more complicated. The material about baptizing a child prior to its birth and the droll argument of the lawyers about whether a mother is her son's relative is quite removed from Sterne's usual characterization of father *Shandy*.

On page 363 the knots motif appears again,[14] with the chambermaid motif. Sterne suggests that instead of devoting a chapter to those subjects, he would rather substitute one on chambermaids, green gowns, and old hats. But the unsettled account of the knots and packages is not forgotten and comes up again near the very end on page 617 as a promise to write a special chapter about knots.

14. Actually, there is no reference to knots on p. 363, but there is a reference to buttonholes; in Russian both are *petlya*. Shklovsky may have been misled by the Russian, or he may have had in mind a more general "fastening" motif. The point makes little difference, however, since Sterne joins both the knot and the buttonhole motifs on p. 617. *Ed. note.*

The references to Jenny are another motif which runs through the novel. Jenny first appears in this way:

> it is no more than a week from this very day, in which I am now writing this book for the edification of the world,—which is *March 9, 1759,*— that my dear, dear *Jenny* observing I look'd a little grave, as she stood cheapening a silk of five-and-twenty shillings a yard,—told the mercer, she was sorry she had given him so much trouble;—and immediately went and bought herself a yard-wide stuff of ten-pence a yard [p. 44].

On pages 48 and 49 Sterne plays with the reader's curiosity concerning the kind of relationship that exists between Jenny and the narrator.

> I own the tender appellation of my dear, dear *Jenny,*—with some other strokes of conjugal knowledge, interspersed here and there, might, naturally enough, have misled the most candid judge in the world into such a determination against me.—All I plead for, in this case, Madam, is strict justice, and that you do so much of it, to me as well as to yourself,—as not to prejudge or receive such an impression of me, till you have better evidence, than I am positive, at present, can be produced against me:—Not that I can be so vain or unreasonable, Madam, as to desire you should therefore think, that my dear, dear *Jenny* is my kept mistress;—no,—that would be flattering my character in the other extream, and giving it an air of freedom, which, perhaps, it has no kind of right to. All I contend for, is the utter impossibility for some volumes, that you, or the most penetrating spirit upon earth, should know how this matter really stands.—It is not impossible, but that my dear, dear *Jenny*! tender as the appellation is, may be my child.—Consider,—I was born in the year eighteen.—Nor is there any thing unnatural or extravagant in the supposition, that my dear *Jenny* may be my friend.—Friend!—My friend. Surely, Madam, a friendship between the two sexes may subsist, and be supported without—Fy! Mr. *Shandy*:—Without anything, Madam, but that tender and delicious sentiment, which ever mixes in friendship, where there is a difference of sex.

The Jenny motif appears again on page 337:

> I shall never get all through in five minutes, that I fear—and the thing I *hope* is, that your worships and reverences are not offended—if you are, depend upon't I'll give you something, my good gentry, next year,

to be offended at—that's my dear *Jenny's* way—but who my *Jenny* is—
and which is the right and which the wrong end of a woman, is the
thing to be *concealed*—it will be told you the next chapter but one, to
my chapter of button-holes,—and not one chapter before.

And on page 493: "I love the Pythagoreans (much more than ever
I dare tell my dear *Jenny*)." There are other references to Jenny on
pages 550 and 610 through 611. This last (I have let several pass)
has a sentimentality seldom equalled in Sterne:

> I will not argue the matter: Time wastes too fast: every letter I
> trace tells me with what rapidity Life follows my pen; the days and
> hours of it, more precious, my dear *Jenny*! than the rubies about thy
> neck, are flying over our heads like light clouds of a windy day, never
> to return more—every thing presses on—whilst thou art twisting that
> lock,—see! it grows grey; and every time I kiss thy hand to bid adieu,
> and every absence which follows it, are preludes to that eternal
> separation which we are shortly to make.—
> —Heaven have mercy upon us both!

> CHAP. IX.

> Now, for what the world thinks of that ejaculation—I would not
> give a groat.

and so ends Chapter 9.[15]

A few words about sentimentality in general are appropriate here.
Sentimentality cannot serve as the mainstay of art, since art has no
mainstay. The presentation of things from "a sentimental point of
view" is a special method of presentation, like the presentation of
them from the point of view of a horse (as in Tolstoy's "Kholstomer")
or of a giant (as in Swift's *Gulliver's Travels*).

Art is essentially trans-emotional, as in stories told of persons
rolled into the sea in a barrel spiked inside like an iron maiden. In
the Russian version of "Tom Thumb"[16] children will not permit the
omission even of the detail of the cannibal cutting off the heads of
his daughters, not because children are cruel, but because the detail
is part of the legend. Professor Anichkov's *Ceremonial Songs of Spring*
includes vernal dancing songs which deal with ugly, quarrelsome

15. Shklovsky mistakenly has, "And so ends Chapter 8." *Ed. note.*
16. "Malchik s palchik," a Russian variant of the Tom Thumb story. *Ed. note.*

husbands; maggots; and death. Although these are unpleasant, they are part of the songs. Gore in art is not necessarily gory; it rhymes with *amor*—it is either the substance of the tonal structure or material for the construction of figures of speech.

Art, then, is unsympathetic—or beyond sympathy—except where the feeling of compassion is evoked as material for the artistic structure. In discussing such emotion we have to examine it from the point of view of the composition itself, in exactly the same way that a mechanic must examine a driving belt to understand the details of a machine; he certainly would not study the driving belt as if he were a vegetarian.

Of course, even Sterne is beyond sympathy, as I shall show. The elder Shandy's son Bobby died at his home the very moment the father was deciding whether to use money, which he had acquired accidentally, either for sending his son abroad or for improving his estate:

> my uncle *Toby* hummed over the letter.
>
> ——— ——— ——— ——— ——— ——— ——— ———
> ——— ——— ——— ——— ——— ——— ——— ———
> ——— ——— ——— ——— ——— ——— ——— —he's
> gone! said my uncle *Toby*.—Where—Who? cried my father.—My nephew, said my uncle *Toby*.—What—without leave—without money —without governor? cried my father in amazement. No:—he is dead, my dear brother, quoth my uncle *Toby* [p. 350].

Sterne here has used death to put his characters at "cross-purposes," a common literary device using two persons talking about two different things and thinking they are talking about one and the same thing. Gogol uses the device in *The Inspector General*, in the first conversation between the Mayor and Khlestakov:

MAYOR: Pardon me—

KH.: Not at all.

MAYOR: As Chief Magistrate of this town, my duty is to see that neither transients nor people of standing are oppressed. . . .

KH.: (first stammering a bit, then towards the end speaking quite loudly) What can be done? . . . It's not my fault. . . . Really, I shall pay. . . . They're sending me some money from home.

(Bobchinsky stares in at the door.) He is far more to blame than I; the beef he serves me is as tough as a board and the devil knows what he puts in his soups—I just had to throw some out the window. He starves me for days. And such odd tea! it smells like fish, not tea. Why should I? ... It's unheard of!

MAYOR: (taken aback) Forgive me, really, I'm not to blame. The beef I inspect at the markets is always good; it's brought in by reliable merchants, sober, well-behaved people. I wouldn't know where his comes from. But if things are not just as they should be, then ... let me suggest that you accompany me to other quarters.

KH.: No, I'd rather not. I know those "other quarters"—the jail. And just what kind of authority do you have? ... How dare you? I ... I work at Petersburg! (Acting boldly) I ... I ... I ...

MAYOR: (aside) Oh! Good Lord, how angry he is. He knows everything; those damned shopkeepers have told him everything.

KH.: (blustering) Even if you come here with all your men, I won't go. I'll go directly to the Prime Minister! (Pounding the table) Who do you think you are? Who?

MAYOR: (Standing at attention, his whole body trembling) Please, don't ruin me. My wife! My little children! Don't set misfortune on a man!

KH.: No, I don't want to. But still! What's that to me? I should go to prison just because you have a wife and children—that's lovely! (Bobchinsky, peeking through the door and thoroughly frightened, hides.) No. Thanks a lot, but I will not.

MAYOR: (trembling) It's my inexperience, honest to God, my inexperience. The shortage of funds ... judge for yourself— my official salary won't keep me in tea and sugar. And if I have taken anything, they were the smallest trifles. Something for the table, enough cloth for a suit. About that corporal's widow who runs a shop and whom I'm said to have flogged— that is slander, by God, slander. It's from people who think evil of me, people ready to take my life.

KH.: So what? They are nothing to me. (Thoughtfully.) Yet I don't know why you talk of those who wish you ill and of some corporal's widow or other. A corporal's wife is something quite different. But you dare not flog me. We're a long way from that. But still . . . . Look at what we have here! I'll pay the bill, but I don't have the cash yet. That's why I'm stuck here, because I don't have a kopeck.

The same talking at cross-purposes occurs in Greboyedov's *Wit Works Woe*:

ZAGORETSKY:	On Chatsky's score this outcry has arisen.
COUNTESS GRANDMOTHER:	Chatsky was escorted out to prison?
ZAGORETSKY:	Was clubbed in the Carpathians, went muzzy from the wound.
COUNTESS GRANDMOTHER:	Has clubbed with the Freemasons and Musselman Mahound?[17]

We find the same technique with the same motivation (deafness) in Russian folk drama, but it arises from a series of puns because of the folk drama's usually loose plot. [A long quotation from the most popular of Russian folk dramas, *Czar Maximilian*, has been omitted here; it consists of one long misunderstanding based upon a series of puns.] These punning misunderstandings are typical of folk drama. Sometimes the device supplants the plot structure itself and leaves the drama without a trace of plot. Roman Jakobson and Peter Bogatyrev analyze the technique in their work on Russian folk themes.[18]

But Sterne's own puns on death do not astonish us as much as the puns made by the father. For Sterne, the death of Bobby Shandy is chiefly motivation for expansion of the material: "Will your worships give me leave to squeeze in a story between these two pages?" (p. 351). And he inserts a fragment from the letter of consolation from Servius Sulpicius Rufus to Cicero. The introduction of this fragment is motivated by what Father Shandy has himself uttered.

17. Trans. by Sir Bernard Pares in *Masterpieces of the Russian Drama*, ed. George Rapall Noyes (New York: Dover Publications, Inc., 1960), I, 133–134. Reprinted through permission of the publisher. *Ed. note*.

18. Roman Jakobson and Peter Bogatyrev, "K probleme razmezhevaniya folkloristiki i literaturovedeniya," ["On the Problem of the Demarcation Between Folklore and Literary Studies"], *Lud Słowianski*, II, No. 2 (1931). *Ed. note*.

Later a collection of classical anecdotes about the disdain of death begins. Curiously, Sterne himself tells of Father Shandy's eloquence:

> My father was as proud of his eloquence as Marcus Tullius Cicero could be for his life, and for aught I am convinced of to the contrary at present, with as much reason: it was indeed his strength—and his weakness too.—His strength—for he was by nature eloquent,—and his weakness—for he was hourly a dupe to it; and provided an occasion in life would but permit him to shew his talents, or say either a wise thing, a witty, or a shrewd one—(bating the case of a systematick misfortune) —he had all he wanted.—A blessing which tied up my father's tongue, and a misfortune which set it loose with good grace, were pretty equal: sometimes, indeed, the misfortune was the better of the two; for instance, where the pleasure of the harangue was as *ten*, and the pain of the misfortune but as *five*—my father gained half in half, and consequently was as well again off, as it never had befallen him [p. 352].

Here Sterne shows with unusual clarity the difference between the "happiness" and "unhappiness" of life taken as an everyday occurrence and as material for art.

Later the mother has to learn about the death of her son. Sterne handles it by having her overhear the news at the door; then he takes it into his head to build a simultaneous action in the kitchen. As I have already pointed out, he plays around with the action while the poor mother is left standing in an uncomfortable pose. At this time, a conversation about the son's death is going on in the study. The thread of conversation has already passed from a discussion of death in general, through a discussion about voyages and the general diffusion of ancient learning (p. 369), and moved on to Socrates' oration before his judges:

> though my mother was a woman of no deep reading, yet the abstract of *Socrates'* oration, which my father was giving my uncle *Toby*, was not altogether new to her.—She listened to it with composed intelligence, and would have done so to the end of the chapter, had not my father plunged (which he had no occasion to have done) into that part of the pleading where the great philosopher reckons up his connections, his alliances, and children; but renounces a security to be so won by working upon the passions of his judges.—"I have friends—I have relations,—I have three desolate children,"—says *Socrates*.—

—Then, cried my mother, opening the door,—you have one more, Mr. *Shandy*, than I know of.

By heaven! I have one less,—said my father, getting up and walking out of the room [p. 370].

Erotic defamiliarization, which is generally presented euphemistically (with genteel wording), is a very important part of Sterne's expansion of the material. I have already treated the basis of this phenomenon in "Art as Technique." In Sterne we find a remarkable diversity of methods of erotic defamiliarization; they are quite numerous, and I shall cite several. I shall begin with one dealing with the recognition of characters:

> I am not ignorant that the *Italians* pretend to a mathematical exactness in their designations of one particular sort of character among them, from the *forte* or *piano* of a certain wind instrument they use,—which they say is infallible.—I dare not mention the name of the instrument in this place;—'tis sufficient we have it amongst us,—but never think of making a drawing by it;—this is aenigmatical, and intended to be so, at least, *ad populum*:—And therefore I beg, Madam, when you come here, that you read on as fast as you can, and never stop to make any inquiry about it[19] [pp. 75–76].

Or here is another:

> Now whether it was physically impossible, with half a dozen hands all thrust into the napkin at a time—but that some one chestnut, of more life and rotundity than the rest, must be put in motion—it so fell out, however, that one was actually sent rolling off the table; and as *Phutatorius* sat straddling under—it fell perpendicularly into that particular aperture of *Phutatorius's* breeches, for which, to the shame and indelicacy of our language be it spoke, there is no chaste word throughout all *Johnson's* dictionary—let it suffice to say—it was that particular aperture, which in all good societies, the laws of decorum do strictly require, like the temple of *Janus* (in peace at least) to be universally shut up [p. 320].

19. "This passage probably alludes, with purposed equivocation, to the Italian *castrati*, some of whom had been imported into England, in the face of considerable popular opposition, to aid in the presentation of operas" (note by James Aiken Work, p. 76). *Ed. note.*

Two further episodes in *Tristram Shandy* are especially typical of Sterne's game of erotic defamiliarization. The two are similar, although one is simply an episode, while the other expands into one of those plots that continually interrupts the others and even becomes one of the major plot strands in the novel. The more important of these is Uncle Toby's wound, a severe wound in the groin. A widow courting him and waiting to marry him does not know whether or not he is castrated and at the same time hesitates to ask. This situation greatly slows the progress of the novel. Sterne comments upon it:

> There is not a greater difference between a single-horse chair and madam *Pompadour's vis-à-vis*, than betwixt a single amour, and an amour thus nobly doubled, and going upon all fours, prancing through-out a grand drama [p. 209].

Hints and allusions repeatedly interrupt the novel. Approximately in Volume VI, Chapter 34, the hints begin to thicken, even though the introductory motif of the journey intrudes. In Volume VII, Chapter 43, Sterne refers to the newly introduced material as if this vein were exhausted:

> I danced it along through *Narbonne, Carcasson,* and *Castle Naudairy,* till at last I danced myself into *Perdrillo's* pavillion, where pulling a paper of black lines, that I might go on straight forwards, without digressions of parenthesis, in my uncle *Toby's* amours—[p. 538].

Thus the wound in the groin and the impossibility of the woman's asking about it in detail is introduced into the romance of Uncle Toby and the widow Wadman as a delaying action. I shall show in several supporting quotations how Sterne impedes the action.

After a solemn promise to continue the story of Toby's amorous adventures without digression, Sterne then delays the action with digressions on digressions tied together by the repetition of such phrases as, "It is with love as with Cuckoldom" (pp. 540, 542). Then come the love metaphors: love is an old hat; love is a pie. The story proceeds with the attacks of the widow Wadman on Uncle Toby, but their description is again interrupted by a long "importunate story," narrated by Trim—"The Story of the King of Bohemia and his seven castles" (pp. 560–569). This story is like the one Sancho Panza tells his master on the night of the adventure with the fulling mill, when he had tied Rosinante's legs. Uncle Toby repeatedly interrupts with remarks on the nature of military techniques and on the style; I have already analyzed the method in *Don Quixote*. Like any "importunate tale," it is based upon the recognition of the stalling tactics. It must be interrupted by a listener. In some cases its function is to hold the flow of the novel in check. Later, Trim abandons his telling of the story of the King of Bohemia and takes up the story of his own love (pp. 568–575); and at last the widow Wadman reappears on the scene. Here the motif of the wound also reappears:

> I am terribly afraid, said widow *Wadman*, in case I should marry him, *Bridget*—that the poor captain will not enjoy his health, with the monstrous wound upon his groin—
> It may not, Madam, be so very large, replied *Bridget*, as you think—and I believe besides, added she—that 'tis dried up—
> —I would like to know—merely for his sake said Mrs. *Wadman*—
> —We'll know the long and the broad of it, in ten days—answered Mrs. *Bridget*, for whilst the captain is paying his addresses to you—I'm confident Mr. Trim will be for making love to me—and I'll let him as much as he will—added *Bridget*—to get it all out of him—[pp. 581–582].

In Volume VIII, Chapter 31, the new material is introduced in the form of a metaphor of the kind frequently found in Sterne. He brings into play the lexically accepted metaphor "hobby-horse" in the sense of a whim and refers it to a real horse, then introduces the "ass" (part of the body) figure of speech. (Perhaps the origin of this metaphor is found in St. Francis of Assisi's phrase about his own body, "My brother ass.") This figure of speech is also developed, and a "situation based on a misconception" is built from it.

The father asks Uncle Toby about his "ass," and the latter thinks this is a euphemistic name for the back part of his anatomy (pp. 583–584). [Shklovsky, apparently misled by the Russian, misinterprets the wordplay here as euphemistic.] A detail of the further development is interesting—Father Shandy's speech to Uncle Toby is nothing other than a parody of the speech of Don Quixote to Sancho Panza about the governorship. I shall not show parallel extracts from both speeches here, especially since the widow Wadman awaits us. Uncle Toby and Trim are going to her, along with Mr. Shandy and his wife, who glance behind them and talk about the coming marriage.

The motif of the impotent husband who has his wife only on the first Sunday of each month crops up again here; the motif had been stated at the very beginning of the novel.

> Unless she should happen to have a child—said my mother—
> But she must persuade my brother *Toby* first to get her one—
> —To be sure, Mr. *Shandy*, quoth my mother.
> —Though if it comes to persuasion—said my father—Lord have mercy upon them.
> Amen: said my mother, *piano*.
> Amen: cried my father, *fortissimè*.
> Amen: said my mother again—but with such a sighing cadence of personal pity at the end of it, as discomfited every fibre about my father—he instantly took out his almanack; but before he could untie it, *Yorick's* congregation coming out of church, became a full answer to one half of his business with it—and my mother telling him it was a sacrament day—left him as little in doubt, as to the other part—He put his almanack into his pocket.
> The first Lord of the Treasury thinking of *ways and means*, could not have returned home, with a more embarrassed look [pp. 613–614].

I let myself quote this passage at length because I want to show how the material Sterne introduces comes not merely from the outside, but rather belongs to one of the threads which tie up all the compositional strands of the novel. Again, as the digressions along the other strands progress, the knot motif reappears (p. 617). At last the wound motif returns, presented, as is typical of Sterne, from the middle:

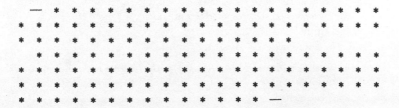

—You shall see the very place, Madam; said my uncle *Toby*.

Mrs. *Wadman* blush'd—look'd towards the door—turn'd pale—blush'd slightly again—recovered her natural colour—blush'd worse than ever; which for the sake of the unlearned reader, I translate thus—

> *"L—d! I cannot look at it—*
> *What would the world say if I look'd at it?*
> *I should drop down, if I look'd at it—*
> *I wish I could look at it—*
> *There can be no sin in looking at it.*
> *—I will look at it"* [p. 623].

But a new development occurs. Uncle Toby thinks the widow is interested in the geographical locality where he was wounded, not in the actual place of the wound on his body. As a result, not even the reader understands the dialogue. The whole movement of the plot is affected here; it is slowed down.

Trim brings a map of Namur (Uncle Toby was wounded at Namur) to the disappointed widow, and once more the play on Uncle Toby's wound is permitted to continue. Sterne repeatedly inserts it into the digressions (pages 625–629). And then comes the famous transposition of time; the previously bypassed Chapters 18 and 19 appear after Chapter 25. The scene resumes with Chapter 26:

> It was just as natural for Mrs. *Wadman*, whose first husband was all his time afflicted with a Sciatica, to wish to know how far from the hip to the groin; and how far she was likely to suffer more or less in her feelings, in the one case than in the other.
>
> She accordingly read *Drake's* anatomy from one end to the other. She had peeped into *Wharton* on the brain, and had borrowed[20] *Graaf* upon the bones and muscles; but could make nothing of it. . . .
>
> To clear up all, she had twice asked Doctor *Slop*, "if poor captain *Shandy* was ever likely to recover of his wound—?"
>
> —He is recovered, Doctor *Slop* would say—
>
> What! quite?
>
> —Quite: madam—

20. This must be a mistake in Mr. *Shandy*; for *Graaf* wrote upon the pancreatick juice, and the parts of generation. *Sterne's note*.

But what do you mean by a recovery? Mrs. *Wadman* would say.
Doctor *Slop* was the worst man alive at definitions [pp. 636–637].

Mrs. Wadman interrogates Captain Shandy himself about the
wound:

> "—Was it without remission?—
> "—Was it more tolerable in bed?
> "—Could he lie on both sides alike with it?
> "—Was he able to mount a horse? [p. 637]

And so on. The business is finally settled when Trim speaks about
Captain Shandy's wound with Bridget, the widow's maid:

> and in this cursed trench, Mrs. *Bridget*, quoth the Corporal, taking her
> by the hand, did he receive the wound which crush'd him so miserable
> *here*—In pronouncing which he slightly press'd the back of her hand
> towards the part he felt for—and let it fall.
> We thought, Mr. *Trim*, it had been more in the middle—said Mrs.
> *Bridget*—
> That would have undone us for ever—said the Corporal.
> —And left my poor mistress undone too—said *Bridget*. . . .
> Come—come—said Bridget—holding the palm of her left-hand
> parallel to the plane of the horizon, and sliding the fingers of the other
> over it, in a way which could not have been done, had there been the
> least wart or protuberance—'Tis every syllable of it false, cried the
> Corporal, before she had half finished the sentence—[p. 639].

It is interesting to compare the symbolism of the hand motions with
the erotic euphemism in the same novel.

A small preliminary observation. For the dramatis personae in
the novel as well as for Sterne himself, the technique of decorous
conversation becomes material for art in the sense that it is a method
of defamiliarization. It is curious that this manual symbolism
occurs in particularly masculine and "obscene" anecdotal folklore
where we know the only rule of decency is the desire to speak as
lewdly as possible. There too we find euphemistic material—in
particular manual symbolism; once again, it is a technique of
defamiliarization.

Let us turn to Sterne and a simple instance of erotic defamiliarization; again I have to quote almost an entire chapter, fortunately a
short one:

> —'Twas nothing,—I did not lose two drops of blood by it—'twas
> not worth calling in a surgeon, had he lived next door to us. . . . The
> chamber-maid had left no ******* *** under the bed:—Cannot you
> contrive, master, quoth *Susannah*, lifting up the sash with one hand, as
> she spoke, and helping me up into the window seat with the other,—
> cannot you manage, my dear, for a single time to **** *** ** ***
> ******?
> I was five years old.—*Susannah* did not consider that nothing was
> well hung in our family,—so slap came the sash down like lightening
> upon us;—Nothing is left,—cried *Susannah*,—nothing is left—for me,
> but to run my country—[p. 376].

She flees to the home of Uncle Toby, who takes the blame in this
case since his servant Trim had removed the hook-leads from the
window sash for casting toy cannons.

Again, this is Sterne's usual technique: He gives the results before
he gives the causes. In this case the cause is given on pages 377–378.
Trim tells the story of the accident, with the aid of hand gestures:

> *Trim*, by the help of his forefinger, laid flat upon the table, and the
> edge of his hand striking a-cross it at right angles, made a shift to tell
> his story so, that priests and virgins might have listened to it;—and the
> story being told,—the dialogue went on as follows [p. 379].

Later, with digressions, discussions of digressions, etc., Sterne
expands an episode about the rumors which spread among the
people concerning what had happened.

It is interesting that Father Shandy, having learned what happened,
runs to his son—with a book—and begins a talk about the general
subject of circumcisions; it is also interesting that at this point Sterne
parodies the motivation of interjected parts:

> —was *Obadiah* enabled to give him a particular account of it, just as it
> had happened.—I thought as much, said my father, tucking up his
> night-gown;—and so walked up stairs.
> One would imagine from this—(though for my own part I some-
> what question it)—that my father before that time, had actually wrote

that remarkable chapter in the *Tristrapædia*, which to me is the most original and entertaining one in the whole book;—and that is the *chapter upon sash-windows*, with a bitter *Philippick* at the end of it, upon the forgetfulness of chamber-maids.—I have but two reasons for thinking otherwise.

First, had the matter been taken into consideration, before the event happened, my father certainly would have nailed up the sash-window for good an' all;—which, considering with what difficulty he composed books,—he might have done with ten times less trouble, than he could have wrote the chapter: this argument I foresee holds good against his writing the chapter, even after the event; but 'tis obviated under the second reason, which I have the honour to offer to the world in support of my opinion, that my father did not write the chapter upon sash-windows and chamber-pots, at the time supposed,—and it is this.

—That, in order to render the *Tristrapædia* complete,—I wrote the chapter myself [pp. 383–384].

I have not even the slightest wish to follow Sterne's novel to the end because that is not what interests me; I am interested, rather, in the theory of the plot. I shall now remark on the abundance of quotations. It certainly would have been possible to have made fuller use of the material introduced in each quotation because almost no technique is represented anywhere in its pure form; but such an approach would have transformed my work into something like an interlinear translation with grammatical remarks. I would have forgotten the material and so exhausted it that I would have deprived the reader of the possibility of understanding it.

In order to follow the course of the novel in my analysis, I have had to show the whole of its "inconsistency." The unusualness of the general plan and the order of the novel, even of the frequently extraordinary handling of the most ordinary elements, is what is characteristic here.

By way of a conclusion and as a demonstration of Sterne's awareness of his work and his exaggerated violations of the usual plot structure, I introduce his very own graphs of the flow of the story of *Tristram Shandy*:

I am now beginning to get fairly into my work; and by the help of a vegitable diet, with a few of the cold seeds, I make no doubt but I shall be able to go on with my uncle *Toby's* story, and my own, in a tolerable straight line. Now,

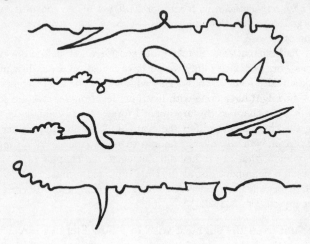

[p. 473] 21

These were the four lines I moved in through my first, second, third, and fourth volumes.—In the fifth volume I have been very good,—the precise line I have described in it being this:

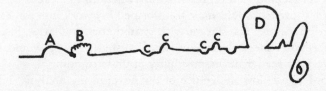

[p. 474]

By which it appears, that except at the curve, marked A. where I took a trip to *Navarre*,—and the indented curve B. which is the short airing when I was there with the Lady *Baussiere* and her page,—I have not taken the least frisk of a digression, till *John de la Casse's* devils led me the round you see marked D.—for as for *c c c c c* they are nothing but parentheses, and the common *ins* and *outs* incident to the lives of the greatest ministers of state; and when compared with what men have

21. These four diagrams are inverted in the Russian text. We have set them aright. *Ed. note.*

done,—or with my own transgressions at the letters A B D—they vanish into nothing [pp. 473–474].

Sterne's diagrams are approximately accurate, but they do not call attention to the crosscurrent of motifs.

The idea of *plot* is too often confused with the description of events—with what I propose provisionally to call the *story*. The story is, in fact, only material for plot formulation. The plot of *Evgeny Onegin* is, therefore, not the romance of the hero with Tatyana, but the fashioning of the subject of this story as produced by the introduction of interrupting digressions. One sharp-witted artist (Vladimir Miklashevsky) proposed to illustrate *Evgeny Onegin* mainly through the digressions (the "small feet," for example); considering it as a composition of motifs, such a treatment would be proper.

The forms of art are explainable by the laws of art; they are not justified by their realism. Slowing the action of a novel is not accomplished by introducing rivals, for example, but by simply *transposing* parts. In so doing the artist makes us aware of the aesthetic laws which underlie both the transposition and the slowing down of the action.

The assertion that *Tristram Shandy* is not a novel is common; for persons who make that statement, opera alone is music—a symphony is chaos.

Tristram Shandy is the most typical novel in world literature.

Victor Shklovsky, Tristram Shandy *Sterna: Stilistichesky kommentary* (Petrograd, 1921).

BORIS TOMASHEVSKY

Thematics

What are the elements involved in narrative art and what is the relationship among those elements? These are the unasked questions behind Boris Tomashevsky's "Thematics." [1] Read not as an exhaustive listing of everything that could possibly get into a narrative, but rather as a suggestive treatment of the methodology of analysis, the essay is thoroughly rewarding. The distinctions Tomashevsky makes and the terminology he has adopted and developed could lead to a profitable study of Western works in a way that has not yet been attempted with any thoroughness.

As a Formalist, Tomashevsky is concerned chiefly with the internal relationships that prevail within the work and secondarily with the literary background of the work. Yet, as Tomashevsky makes clear in the opening pages, literature is not entirely self-contained. For Tomashevsky, as for most Western critics, a work is unified by a theme which runs through it; the theme makes the work cohere. And, like Kenneth Burke, Tomashevsky argues that we interest men by dealing with their interests; selection of a theme, consequently, is a crucial aesthetic problem. A work that does not in some way deal with our recurrent interests simply will not endure. Moreover, he recognizes that we cannot respond to the theme unless the author enlists our emotions; if the author is writing well, he makes us sympathize with what he presents as good and deplore what he presents as evil. But even though the work is based upon our interests and emotions, Tomashevsky (like most modern critics) insists that these do not have free play. If we are responding properly, our feelings are shaped and determined by the work itself.

With this bow to extrinsic criticism quickly made, Tomashevsky turns to more purely formalistic concerns. The central distinction Tomashevsky makes is that between story and plot. [2] Actually, his main concern is plot, for that is where artistry lies; the story is a background against which elements of the plot are studied.

1. We have included here approximately the first half of the essay only.
2. See above, p. 57. Tomashevsky makes approximately the same distinction between plot and story that Shklovsky made, except that the former's analysis of the notions of motif and motivation make the distinction more precise.

Perhaps the most impressive feature of Tomashevsky's essay is its orderly diversity. The author considers everything from the motif—the elementary, atomlike unit of meaning out of which all else is constructed—through the various kinds of "motivation" which determine the choice of particular motifs, to point of view and interrelationships among characters. Perhaps the only comparable piece of criticism easily available to Western readers is Aristotle's Poetics. *Each abstracts the essentials of the genre under discussion and analyzes their possible combinations; each places the "aesthetic ought" above the realistic and the moral by insisting upon a strict structural functionalism; and each, despite occasional evaluative comments, is inductive and descriptive rather than prescriptive.*

Practical critics and scholars can possibly learn much from the "Thematics." One lesson, and one that seems both obvious and especially useful, is the importance of distinguishing among types of motifs and motivations. We too easily assume that whatever gets into a work gets there simply because the author willfully put it in. The distinction between bound motifs (those without which that particular story could not be told) and free motifs (those added by the author for whatever reason) could possibly lead to more meaningful readings of both prose fiction and drama. The distinctions among the various kinds of motivation would have the same result. In discussing either the meaning or the artistry of a narrative it would seem advisable to treat those elements required for the action somewhat differently from those included for other reasons. The fact that Hester, in The Scarlet Letter, *for example, is beautiful seems necessary to make the story plausible, and her cleverness as a seamstress is in part a realistic touch explaining how she made her living. But the woods where Hester and Dimmesdale meet are of a different order; they are required only by Hawthorne's aesthetic and moral imagination. A reading of the story—whether for Hawthorne's world view or for his craft—should give the latter more weight than the former.*

More generally, if we accept the premise that the first step toward understanding a piece of literature is to understand the why of all its parts, Tomashevsky provides a relatively complete conceptual framework and a usable vocabulary.

1. Selection of Themes

The meanings of the separate sentences of a work of literature combine to produce a definite structure unified by a general thought or theme. The theme (what is being said in a work) unites the separate elements of a work. The work as a whole has a theme, and its individual parts also have themes. Anything written in meaningful language has a theme; only intentionally meaningless works, because they are merely experimental laboratory exercises of certain poetic schools, have no themes.

To be coherent, a verbal structure must have a unifying theme running through it. Consequently, both the selection and the development of the theme are important aesthetically.

The effect that a given theme will have on the reader is a significant consideration in its selection. By "reader" we mean a rather indefinite group of persons; often a writer is not sure who will read his work. Nevertheless, the writer always considers the reader, at least abstractly, even if only to try to imagine himself in the reader's place. Such consideration gained acceptance in the kind of classical address to the reader that we find, for example, in the last stanzas of *Evgeny Onegin*:

> Whoever you may have been, O my reader,
> Friend or foe—I wish to part
> With you, for now, as friend.
> Farewell. Whatever you have
> Sought with me here in these careless stanzas,
> Whether wild remembrances,
> Respite from labors,
> Vivid pictures, wit,
> Or grammatical errors,
> God grant that, in this little book,
> You found at least a crumb
> To arouse amusement, inspiration,
> Emotion—or a clamor in the journals.
> Let's part with this. Farewell.

Such consideration for the reader is calculated to arouse his interest.

A work must be interesting, and a writer choosing a theme is guided by the "interest" inherent in that theme. But interest—personal interest in something—takes many forms. Literary craftsmanship is the most immediate interest of writers and of those who read them most closely, and writers and their close readers are certainly the strongest forces in literature. Professionalism, literary novelty, and new techniques have always been the goals of the most progressive literary groups. The writer constantly tries to solve the problem of artistic tradition, which in literary experience is like the encumbrance of an ancestral heirloom. On the other hand, the objective interests of the reader, far removed from problems of literary craftsmanship, may vary from a demand for simple entertainment (satisfaction with "cheap" literature, like the Pinkerton detective stories and Tarzan) to a demand for a combination of literary interests and general cultural concerns.

Here reality—that is, themes that are "real" in the context of contemporary cultural thought—satisfies the reader. Thus each of Turgenev's novels naturally provoked a great deal of journalistic writing which, since it was only slightly concerned with the novels as works of art, attacked the general cultural problems (chiefly social) which the novels had raised. Such journalism was quite legitimate as an answer, a real response, to the themes Turgenev chose.

At present the "real" themes are themes of the revolution and revolutionary life, themes which permeate all the prose of Pilnyak, Ehrenburg, and others, and the poetry of Mayakovsky, Tikhonov, and Aseyev.

Vital issues, current, topical questions—such are the elementary forms of reality. But topical works (feuilletons, satiric songs of musical comedy), precisely because they are topical, last no longer than the temporary interest in the topic. Their themes lack staying power; they are unable to meet the changing, day-to-day interests of the audience. On the other hand, the more significant and long-lasting the theme, the better the guarantee of the life of the work. Enlarging the limits of "reality," we may reach "general human" interests (problems of love and death) which are the fixed bases of the entire course of human history. Yet these general human interests must be developed through some kind of specific material, and if that material is not relevant to reality, the formulation of the problem may prove "uninteresting."

Reality in literature need not be thought of as the representation of contemporary conditions. For example, the current interest in revolution implies that a historical novel from any revolutionary period, or a Utopian novel depicting a revolutionary movement in a fantastic setting, can in essence be related to the times. For instance, the recent run of plays on the Russian stage about the "Time of Troubles" (the works of Ostrovsky, Alexey Tolstoy, Chayev, and others, and now those of Kostomarov) shows that a historical theme from a given period can be made contemporary—that is, can be received with perhaps greater interest than the presentation of what is more obviously contemporary. Finally, within the contemporary period itself one needs to know what to depict. Not everything that is contemporary is essential, and not everything evokes the same interest.

General interest in a theme, then, is determined by the historical conditions prevailing when the work appears; the literary tradition and the problems it poses are among the most important of these historical conditions.

But selection of an interesting theme is not enough. Interest must also be maintained, attention stimulated. The theme does both.

The emotion attached to the theme plays a major role in maintaining interest. There is good reason for classifying works designed to produce a spontaneous effect on masses of listeners (dramatic works, for example) as comedy or tragedy by the emotion they communicate. The emotions a work of art excites are its chief means of holding attention. It is not enough, for example, to state the phases of the revolutionary movement in the cold tones of a lecture; the listener must sympathize, must be indignant, joyful, disturbed. Only then does the work become *really* "real"; only then are the listener's emotions unprotestingly led in the desired direction. Most poetry is built on sympathy and aversion, on the evaluation of the material as it is presented. In literary works the conventional virtuous hero and the villain directly express this positive or negative evaluation. Because the feelings and emotions of the reader must be oriented, the theme of a work is usually emotionally colored; it evokes and develops feelings of hostility or sympathy according to a system of values.

But we must not forget that this emotional coloration is inherent in the work; it is not imposed by the reader. We cannot question whether a certain kind of hero (Lermontov's Pechorin,[3] for example)

3. The protagonist of *A Hero of Our Time. Ed. note.*

is negative or positive; we must rather analyze that emotional reaction in its context (and even the context may not express the personal opinion of the author). This emotional coloration, which is readily apparent in unsophisticated literary genres (the adventure novel, for example, with its rewards for virtue and vice) may be so subtle and intricate in more complex works, or in other cases so confused, that it cannot be expressed in a simple formula. Nevertheless, the function of sympathy is primarily to direct interest and maintain attention—to call forth, as it were, the personal interest of the reader in the development of the theme.

2. STORY AND PLOT

A theme has a certain unity and is composed of small thematic elements arranged in a definite order.

We may distinguish two major kinds of arrangement of these thematic elements: (1) that in which causal-temporal relationships exist between the thematic elements, and (2) that in which the thematic elements are contemporaneous, or in which there is some shift of theme without internal exposition of the causal connections. The former are *stories* (tales, novels, epics); the latter have no "story," they are "descriptive" (e.g., descriptive and didactic poems, lyrics, and travel books such as Karamzin's *Letters of a Russian Traveller* or Goncharov's *The Frigate Pallas*).

We must emphasize that a story requires not only indications of time, but also indications of cause. Time indicators may occur in telling about a journey, but if the account is only about the sights and not about the personal adventures of the travelers, we have exposition without story. The weaker the causal connection, the stronger the purely chronological connection. As the story line becomes weaker, we move from the novel to the chronicle, to a simple statement of the sequence of events (*The Childhood Years of Bagrov's Grandson*[4]).

Let us take up the notion of the story, the aggregate of mutually related events reported in the work. No matter how the events were originally arranged in the work and despite their original order of

4. A volume of reminiscences by Sergey Aksakov, published in 1858. *Ed. note.*

introduction, in practice the story may be told in the actual chronological and causal order of events.

Plot is distinct from story. Both include the same events, but in the plot the events *are arranged* and connected according to the orderly sequence in which they were presented in the work.[5]

The idea expressed by the theme is the idea that *summarizes* and unifies the verbal material in the work. The work as a whole may have a theme, and at the same time each part of a work may have its own theme. The development of a work is a process of diversification unified by a single theme. Thus Pushkin's "The Shot" develops the story of the narrator's meetings with Silvio and the Count, and the story of the conflict between the two men. The story of life in the regiment and the country is developed, followed by the first part of the duel between Silvio and the Count, and the story of their final encounter.

After reducing a work to its thematic elements, we come to parts that are irreducible, the smallest particles of thematic material: "evening comes," "Raskolnikov kills the old woman," "the hero dies," "the letter is received," and so on. The theme of an irreducible part of a work is called the *motif*; each sentence, in fact, has its own motif.

It should be noted that the meaning of "motif," as used in historical poetics—in comparative studies of migratory plots (for example, in the study of the *skaz* [or yarn][6])—differs radically from its meaning here, although they are usually considered identical. In comparative studies a motif is a thematic unit which occurs in various works (for example, "the abduction of the bride," "the helpful beast"—that is, the animal that helps the hero solve his problem—etc.). These motifs move in their entirety from one plot to another. In comparative poetics, reduction to the smaller elements

5. In brief, the story is "the action itself," the plot, "how the reader learns of the action."

6. Possibly the nearest equivalent of *skaz* is "yarn." Technically, a *skaz* is a story in which the manner of telling (the normal speech patterns of the narrator—dialect, pronunciation, grammatical peculiarities, pitch patterns, etc.) is as important to the effect as the story itself. For a description of the American equivalent of the *skaz*, see Samuel Clemens' widely reprinted "How to Tell a Story." *Ed. note.*

is not important; what is important is only that within the limits of
the given genre these "motifs" are always found in their complete
forms. Consequently, in comparative studies one must speak of
motifs that have remained intact historically, that have preserved
their unity in passing from work to work, rather than of "irreducible"
motifs. Nevertheless, many motifs of comparative poetics remain
significant precisely because they are also motifs in our theoretical
sense.

Mutually related motifs form the thematic bonds of the work.
From this point of view, the story is the aggregate of motifs in their
logical, causal-chronological order; the plot is the aggregate of those
same motifs but having the relevance and the order which they had
in the original work. The place in the work in which the reader
learns of an event, whether the information is given by the author,
or by a character, or by a series of indirect hints—all this is irrelevant
to the story. But the aesthetic function of the plot is precisely this
bringing of an arrangement of motifs to the attention of the reader.
Real incidents, not fictionalized by an author, may make a story.
A plot is wholly an artistic creation.

Usually there are different kinds of motifs within a work. By
simply retelling the story we immediately discover what may be
omitted without destroying the coherence of the narrative and what
may not be omitted without disturbing the connections among
events. The motifs which cannot be omitted are *bound motifs*; those
which may be omitted without disturbing the whole causal-
chronological course of events are *free motifs*.

Although only the bound motifs are required by the story, free
motifs (digressions, for example) sometimes dominate and determine
the construction of the plot. These incidental motifs (details, etc.)
are presented so that the tale may be told artistically; we shall return
later to the various functions they perform. Literary tradition largely
determines the use of free motifs, and each literary school has its
characteristic stock; however, bound motifs are usually distinguished
by their "vitality"—that is, they appear unchanged in the works of
various schools. Nevertheless, literary tradition clearly plays a
significant role in the development of the story (for example, the
stories of typical novels of the 1840's and '50's are about the disasters

of a petty official—e.g., Gogol's "The Greatcoat," Dostoevsky's *Poor People*; in the 1820's the stories were usually about the unfortunate love of a European for a foreigner—e.g., Pushkin's *Captive of the Caucasus* and *The Gypsies*).

In "The Undertaker" Pushkin wrote pointedly about the use of free motifs within a literary tradition:

> Just at noon the next day, the coffin maker and his daughters left through the wicket side-gate of their newly purchased home and set off for a neighbor's. I shall not begin to describe either the Russian kaftan of Adrian Prokhorovich nor the European clothes of Akulina or Darya —differing in that respect from the usual notions of recent novelists. I suppose, however, that it is not superfluous to note that both children wore the yellow caps and red shoes that they customarily wear only on festive occasions.

The description of the clothes is remarked upon here as a traditional free motif of that period (the 1830's).

Among the various kinds of motifs we may distinguish a special class of introductory motifs which require specific supplementation by other motifs, as, typically, when the hero is given a task. For example: A father wants his daughter to marry; the daughter, to avoid the marriage, assigns an impossible task. Or the hero woos the princess who, to avoid the dreaded marriage, sets him a task which at first seems impossible; or, as in Pushkin's "Tale of Balda," the priest, in order to rid himself of a worker, commissions him to collect quitrent from the devil. Any embodiment of this task motif requires an account of the task itself, an account which also serves to introduce the story of the hero's exploits. The delay of the story is another such motif; in *The Arabian Nights* Scheherazade forestalls her execution by telling stories to the prince who threatens to take her life. This "story telling" motif is the device which introduces the tales. So also in adventure stories there are motifs of pursuit, and so on. Usually the introduction of a free motif occurs as a development of a previously introduced motif which is inherently bound up with the story.

Motifs may be also classified according to their objective functions.

Usually a story is developed by introducing several characters (dramatis personae) related to each other by mutual interests or by other ties (kinship, for example). This interrelationship at any given moment is the *situation*. For cxample, the hero loves the heroine, but she loves his rival. We have three characters: hero, heroine, rival. These are the ties: the love of the hero for the heroine and her love for the rival. Also typical are situations in which the characters are related by opposition, in which different persons want to change a situation by different means. For example, the hero loves the heroine and she loves him, but the parents prevent their marriage; they try to marry, the parents try to separate them.

A story may be thought of as a journey from one situation to another. During the journey a new character may be introduced (complicating the situation), old characters eliminated (for example, by the death of the rival), or the prevailing relationships changed.

Motifs which change the situation are *dynamic motifs*; those which do not are *static*. Consider, for example, Pushkin's "Mistress into Maid." Although Alexey Berestov loves Akulina, his father is arranging his marriage to Liza Muromskaya. Alexey, unaware that Akulina and Liza are one and the same person, objects to the marriage thrust upon him by his father. He goes to have it out with Liza and discovers that she is Akulina, so the situation changes— Alexey's objections to the marriage vanish. The discovery that Akulina and Liza are the same person is a dynamic motif.

Free motifs are usually static, but not all static motifs are free. Thus we assume that if a murder is necessary to the progress of the story, one of the characters must have a revolver. The motif of the revolver, as the reader becomes aware of it, is both static and bound—bound because without the revolver the murder could not be committed. This situation occurs in Ostrovsky's *The Poor Bride*.

Descriptions of nature, local color, furnishings, the characters, their personalities, and so on—these are typically static motifs. The actions and behavior of the main characters are typically dynamic motifs.

Dynamic motifs are motifs which are central to the story and which keep it moving; in the plot, on the other hand, static motifs may predominate.

From the point of view of the story, motifs are easily ranked according to their importance. Dynamic motifs are most important, then motifs which prepare their way, then motifs defining the situation, and so on. The relative importance of a motif to the story may be determined by retelling the *story* in abridged form, then comparing the abridgement with the more fully developed narrative.

The development of a story may generally be understood as a progress from one situation to another, so that each situation is characterized by a *conflict* of interest, by discord and struggle among the characters.[7] The dialectical development of the story is analogous to the development of social-historical processes in which each new historical stage is seen both as a result of the struggle of social groups in the preceding stage and as a battlefield for the interests of the new social group constituting the current social system.

The struggle among the characters (the conflicts of interests mentioned above) is accompanied both by the gathering of the characters into groups and by the agreement of each group upon the tactics to be used against the other. This conduct of the struggle— the aggregate of motifs which characterize it—is called the *intrigue* (the usual term in dramatic criticism).

The development of the intrigue (or, with complex groups of characters, parallel intrigues) leads either to the elimination of the conflicts or to the creation of new conflicts. Usually at the end of the story all the conflicts are reconciled and the interests harmonized. If a situation containing the conflict furthers the progress of the story, then, since the coexistence of two conflicting forces is impossible, one must inevitably prevail. The later harmonious situation, which does not require further development, will neither evoke nor arouse the reader's anticipation. That is why the condition at the end of a work is so static. This static condition is called the *ending*.[8] Thus the old moralistic novels usually have a double movement in

7. Quite the same happens if, in place of a group of characters, we have a psychological novel in which the internal psychic history of the hero is described. The various psychological motifs of his conduct, the various sides of his spiritual life, instincts, passions, etc., assume the role usually played by other characters. In this respect we can generalize about his whole past and future.

8. To put this in more familiar terminology, the ending occurs after all tensions have been eased. Tomashevsky's analysis of plot structure here follows closely Aristotle's analysis of dramatic structure. A study of the "Thematics" as Aristotle's *Poetics* brought up to date would be enlightening. *Ed. note.*

which virtue is oppressed while vice triumphs (a moral conflict), but in the ending virtue is rewarded and vice punished.

Sometimes a harmonious situation is found at the beginning of stories in which, for example, "the hero had been living peacefully and quietly. Suddenly . . . etc." Here, in order to get the story going, a dynamic motif destroys the initial peaceful situation. The aggregate of such motifs, disturbing the tranquillity of the initial situation and provoking action, is called the *exciting force*. Usually the nature of the exciting force determines the whole course of the story, and all the intrigue is reducible only to the various motifs which determine the basic conflict introduced by the exciting force. This change is the *peripety* (the movement from one situation to another).

The more complicated the conflict within the situation and the stronger the opposing interests of the characters, the greater the *tension* of situation. The increase in tension is proportionate to the proximity of a great change of fortune. Tension is usually achieved by preparing for the change in the situation. Thus in the typical adventure novel the villain, seeking to destroy the hero, constantly has the odds in his favor. He prepares for the hero's defeat, but at the last possible moment, when the hero's downfall seems positively certain, he is unexpectedly saved and the machinations of his enemies frustrated. Such preparation increases the tension.

Tension usually reaches its highest point just before the ending. This culminating point of the tension is usually called the climax [*Spannung*]. In the simplest system of dialectics relevant to the construction of a story, the climax is like the antithesis (the thesis is the exciting force, the antithesis the climax, and the synthesis the ending).

We must remember that the formation of a plot from the material of the story requires a narrative introduction to the initial situation. The presentation of circumstances determining the initial cast of characters and their interrelationships is called the *exposition*.

Not all narratives begin with an exposition.[9] In the simplest case—

9. From the point of view of the arrangement of the narrative material, the part beginning the narrative is called the *prologue*. The close is called the *epilogue*. The prologue may include neither the exposition nor the exciting force, just as the epilogue may not occur simultaneously with the outcome of the theme.

that in which the author opens by acquainting us with the elements of the story material—we have *immediate exposition*. But the quick start (*ex abrupto*), in which the presentation begins with previously developed events and we are only gradually acquainted with the situation of the hero, is also fairly common. In such cases we have *delayed exposition*, which is sometimes quite prolonged. We may distinguish among the introductory motifs which comprise the exposition. Sometimes we come to know the situation through hints, and only the assimilation of such seemingly incidental remarks forms a coherent impression; then we do not have exposition proper —that is, the expository motifs are not grouped into one complete narrative section.

But sometimes, when outlining a certain event whose general ramifications we do not yet understand, the author, in clarifying it (either through his own comments or through the speech of a character) will include expository material which tells us about what has already happened. Then we have *transposed exposition*; more specifically, we have a time shift in the elaboration of the story material.

Delayed exposition may be continued to the very end, so that throughout the whole narrative the reader sometimes does not know all that is necessary for understanding what happens. Usually the author withholds information about the circumstances involving a group of major characters, telling the reader only what one or the other of the characters knows. The information about these "un-revealed" circumstances is then given in the ending. Such an ending, including in itself elements of exposition and, as it were, casting light back on everything preceding the peripety, is called a *regressive ending*. Let us assume that neither the reader of Pushkin's "Mistress into Maid" nor the hero, Alexey Berestov, knows the identity of Akulina and Liza Muromskaya. In that event, information about that identity would have regressive force—that is, it would give a true and fresh understanding of all the preceding situations. "Snowstorm," also from Pushkin's *Tales of Belkin*, is so constructed.

Usually this delayed exposition begins as a series of hints. In that case, these combinations are possible: The reader knows, the main characters do not; some of the characters know, some do not; the reader and some of the characters do not know; no one knows (the truth is discovered by accident); the characters know, but the reader does not.

These hints may run throughout the narrative and may involve only some of the motifs. In such a case the same motif may appear several times in the construction of the plot. Consider a typical novelistic device: One of the characters, long before the time of the action, has been kidnaped (first motif). A character appears, and we learn from his biography that he was not raised by his parents and does not know them (second motif). Then we learn (usually by comparison of dates and circumstances, or by the motif of a sign— an amulet, a birthmark, etc.) that the kidnaped child and the hero are the same person. Thus the identity of the first and second motifs is established. This repetition of a motif in variant forms is typical of plots in which aspects of the story are not introduced in their natural chronological order. A repeated motif usually shows the connection which exists in the story between parts of the plot structure. Thus, if, in the typical example used above, the means of recognizing the lost child is an amulet, then this amulet motif accompanies both the narrative about the disappearance of the child and the biography of the new character. (See, for example, Ostrovsky's *The Guilty Are Without Blame.*)

Such connecting motifs make chronological displacements possible in narratives.[10] Exposition is not the only element that may be transposed; certain parts of the story may be narrated after the reader knows that they have already occurred. A coherent account of significant *parts* of an event which foretells what will happen in an episode before it is narrated is called foreshadowing [*Vorgeschichte*]. Delayed exposition, or the presentation of the biography of a new character introduced into a new situation, are typical forms of foreshadowing. Many examples of the technique may be found in Turgenev's novels. "Premonition" [*Nachgeschichte*], an account of

10. If the motif is repeated more or less frequently, and especially if it is a free motif—that is, not involved in the story, then it is called a *leitmotif*. Thus certain characters appearing in the narrative under various disguises are often accompanied by some kind of fixed motif so that the reader may recognize them.

what will happen told prior to the approaching events to prepare the reader, is more rare. *Nachgeschichte* sometimes takes the form of auguries, predictions, or of more or less likely assumptions.

The narrator plays a major role in the indirect development of the story materials because plot shifts are common functions of the narrative style.

Kinds of narrators may be distinguished: Either the tale is told objectively by the author as a simple report, without an explanation of how the events became known (the *objective* tale), or else it is told by a designated narrator who functions as a relatively specific character. Sometimes the narrator is presented as a person who hears the story from someone else (Pushkin's "The Shot" and "The Stationmaster"), or as a more or less involved witness, or finally as one of the participants in the action (the hero in Pushkin's *The Captain's Daughter*). Sometimes the "listener" or witness is not the narrator, and in the objective story his knowledge may be recorded although he plays no part in the narrative (Maturin's *Melmoth the Wanderer*). Or sometimes complicated methods of narration are used (for example, in *The Brothers Karamazov* the narrator is presented as a witness to the action although he does not appear in the novel and the entire story is told objectively).

Thus two basic types of narration exist—the *omniscient* and the *limited*. In the omniscient, the author knows everything, including the hidden thoughts of the characters; in the limited the whole tale is filtered through the mind of the narrator (a person in a position to know) and each piece of information is accompanied by an explanation of how and when he learned about it.

Mixed systems are possible. Usually in omniscient narration the narrator traces the fate of a particular character, and we consequently learn what that character did and knew. Then he is abandoned, attention passes to another character, and we are told what this new character did and knew. Thus the "hero" himself is frequently a kind of narrative thread—that is, covertly he is the narrator; and even as the author himself tells us about him, he also takes pains to communicate only what his hero could tell. Sometimes the structure of the work is determined only by fastening the thread of the story to this or that character. Should the author follow the fate of other characters, then the hero may change even though the story material remains the same.

As an example, let us discuss the fairy tale "The Caliph Stork," as told by [Wilhelm] Hauff. Here is a brief summary: Once the Caliph Khacid and his vizier bought from a peddler a snuffbox which contained a secret powder and a message written in Latin. The learned vizier Selim read the message, which stated that a pinch of the secret powder and pronunciation of the word *mutabor* would turn them into any animal. But if they laughed while they were transformed, the word would be forgotten and it would be impossible to change back into human form. The Caliph and the vizier changed themselves into storks, and at their very first meeting with other storks they burst out laughing. The word was forgotten. The storks—the Caliph and the vizier—were doomed to remain birds forever. Flying over Bagdad, they saw a commotion in the street and heard cries reporting that a certain Mizra, son of the most wicked enemy of Khacid—the magician Kashnur—had seized power. The storks then took flight, intending to visit the grave of the Prophet to free themselves from the sorcery. On the way they stopped to spend the night in some ruins, where they met an owl which spoke to them in human language and told them that it had been the only daughter of an Indian prince. The magician Kashnur, who had sought her for his son Mizra to marry but had been refused, had then stolen into her palace in the form of a Negro, given her the magic potion which changed her into an owl, and carried her to these ruins, telling her that she would remain so until someone agreed to marry her. But also, as a child she had heard the prediction that storks would bring her good fortune. She agreed to tell the Caliph how to free himself from the curse on the condition that he promise to marry her. The Caliph agreed after some hesitation, and the owl led him into a room in which the sorcerers had gathered. There the Caliph overheard Kashnur's story, from which he learned how the peddler had deceived him. During the telling he recognized the forgotten word, *mutabor*. The Caliph and the owl were transformed again into people, and all returned to Bagdad, where they avenged themselves on Mizra and Kashnur.

The tale is called "The Caliph Stork"—that is, the hero is the Caliph Khacid because the author follows his fate throughout the narrative. The history of the princess-owl is introduced as she tells her story to the Caliph when they meet at the ruins.

It is quite easy to change the arrangement of the material in order to follow the fate of the heroine; then it would be necessary to tell her tale first and to introduce the history of the Caliph by having him tell his tale before the removal of the spell. The story remains the same, but the plot is altered substantially because the narrative thread is changed.

The transfer of motifs deserves mention—the motif of the peddler and the motif of Kashnur, Mizra's father, develop into the same motif when the Caliph-stork overhears the magician. The fact that the transformation of the Caliph is the result of Kashnur's intrigue is given at the end of the tale, not at the beginning, as would be the case in a cause-and-effect presentation.

Two things here pertain to the story: (1) the history of the Caliph, deceived by Kashnur's magic; and (2) the history of the princess, enchanted by Kashnur. These two parallel lines of the story cross when the Caliph and the princess meet and come to an agreement. The story continues then along a single thread—their liberation and the punishment of the sorcerer.

The structure of the plot depends upon the order of events as we follow the fate of the Caliph. Covertly, the Caliph is the narrator—that is, in the objective presentation of the tale the information is given in the order in which the Caliph would learn of it. This determines the entire structure of the fantastic plot. The example is typical, for usually the hero is a covert (potential) narrator. This explains why one frequently finds that the structure of the novel often tends to take the form of a memoir—that is, the hero himself is compelled to tell his own story. This technique is tantamount to revealing the devices used in following the action of the hero and thereby justifies the introduction of certain information and the order of the motifs.

In analyzing the plot structure of individual works, attention should also be given to the use of *time* and *place* in the narrative.

Story time and *reading time* are distinct in a work of art. Story time is the amount of time required by the events that are said to occur; reading time is the time required for reading the work (or witnessing the spectacle). The latter depends on the "size" of the work.

Story time is given in three ways: (1) The moment of action may be dated absolutely (when the chronological moment is simply stated—for example, "at two o'clock on January 8 in 18—" or "in winter"), or relatively (by indicating the simultaneity of events or their chronological relationship—e.g., "after two years," etc.); (2) the duration of events may be indicated ("the conversation lasted for half an hour," "the journey continued for three months," or indirectly, "after five days they arrived at the appointed place"); and (3) an impression of the duration of time may be given, so that we indirectly determine the passage of time by judging the length of the speech or the normal duration of the action. We may note that writers use the last most freely, cramming long speeches into short lines and, conversely, expanding short speeches and quick action into long durations of time.

The place of the action may be either *static* or *dynamic*. If static, all the characters gather in one place (which is why hotels or their equivalents so frequently figure in stories—they make unexpected meetings possible); if dynamic, the characters are moved from place to place for the necessary encounters (travel-type tales, for example).

3. MOTIVATION

The system of motifs comprising the theme of a given work must show some kind of artistic unity. If the individual motifs, or a complex of motifs, are not sufficiently suited to the work, if the reader feels that the relationship between certain complexes of motifs and the work itself is obscure, then that complex is said to be superfluous. If all the parts of the work are badly suited to one another, the work is *incoherent*. That is why the introduction of each separate motif or complex of motifs must be *motivated*. The network of devices justifying the introduction of individual motifs or of groups of motifs is called *motivation*.

The devices of motivation are so numerous and varied that they must be classified:

(1) The principle of *compositional motivation* refers to the economy and usefulness of the motifs. Separate motifs may characterize either

objects (stage properties) brought to the reader's attention or the activities of the characters (episodes). Not a single property may remain unused in the telling, and no episode may be without influence on the situation. Chekhov referred to just such compositional motivation when he stated that if one speaks about a nail beaten into a wall at the beginning of a narrative, then at the end the hero must hang himself on that nail.

A prop, in this case a weapon, is used in precisely this way in Ostrovsky's *The Poor Bride*. The third act set includes "a revolver hung on the tapestry over the divan." At first this detail of the setting seems a simple, concrete feature characterizing Karandyshev's way of life. In the sixth scene attention is directed towards this detail:

ROBINSON: (looking at the tapestry)   What do you have here?

KARANDYSHEV: Cigars.

R.:   No, what's hanging up there? Is this real?

K.:   What do you mean "real"? This is a Turkish weapon.

The dialogue continues and the speakers ridicule the weapon; then the motif narrows until a remark is made about the worthlessness of the pistol:

K.:   But in what way is it worthless? This pistol, for example . . . (he takes the pistol from the wall).

PARATOV: (taking the pistol from him)   This pistol?

K.:   Ah, be careful—it shoots.

P.:   Don't be afraid. It's just as dangerous whether it fires or not. All the same, it won't fire. Shoot at me from five paces; I'll let you.

K.:   Well—no. This pistol may be loaded.

P.:   So—it will do to hammer nails into the wall.
            (Throws the pistol on the table.)

At the end of the act the fleeing Karandyshev takes the pistol from the table; in the fourth act he shoots Larissa with it.

Here compositional considerations motivate the introduction of the pistol motif. Because it prepares the audience for the final moments of the play, the pistol is an indispensable part of the denouement. This is the first kind of compositional motivation. A second type of compositional motivation occurs when motifs are used as devices of characterization, but these motifs must be appropriate to the story. Thus in the same play, *The Poor Bride*, the motif of the burgundy prepared and adulterated by a shady wine merchant for cheap sale typifies the poverty of Karandyshev's daily life and prepares for the departure of Larissa.

Details which show character may be integrated with the action either by psychological analogy (e.g., moonlight nights for love scenes and lightning and thunder for scenes of death or evil in novels) or by contrast (the motif of indifferent nature). In *The Poor Bride*, when Larissa dies, the singing of a Gypsy chorus is heard from the restaurant door.

We have still to consider the possibility of misleading motivation; props and episodes may be used to distract the reader's attention from the real situation. This happens frequently in detective novels, where a series of details is given in order to lead the reader (and a group of characters—for example, Watson or the police in Conan Doyle) up a blind alley. The author forces the reader to expect an ending inconsistent with the facts of the case. Techniques of misleading motivation occur chiefly in works created against the background of a major literary tradition; the reader naturally interprets each detail according to the conventions of the tradition. The deception is discovered at the end, and the reader is convinced that all such details were introduced merely to support the final surprises.

Misleading motivation (the play upon generally known literary rules firmly entrenched in tradition and used by the author in other than their traditional ways) is indispensable for parody.

(2) *Realistic motivation.* We demand an element of "illusion" in any work. No matter how convention-filled and artistic it is, our perception of it must be accompanied by a feeling that what happens in it is "real." The naive reader feels this with extraordinary force and may try to verify the authenticity of the statements, perhaps even to make certain that the characters existed. Pushkin, after completing *The History of the Pugachyov Rebellion*, published *The Captain's Daughter* in the form of the memoirs of Grinyov and concluded with this epilogue:

The manuscript of Peter Andreyevitch Grinyov was given to us by one of his grandchildren who had learned that we were occupied with a work concerning the times his grandfather described. We decided, with the family's permission, to publish it separately.

Pushkin creates the illusion of a real Grinyov and his memoirs, supported in detail by a well-known personal fact of Pushkin's life—his historical study of the history of Pugachyov. The illusion is further supported by the opinions and convictions expressed by Grinyov, which differ in many ways from opinions expressed by Pushkin himself.

For more experienced readers the need for realistic illusion expresses itself as a demand for "lifelikeness." Although firmly aware of the fictitious nature of the work, the experienced reader nevertheless demands some kind of conformity to reality, and finds the value of the work in this conformity. Even readers fully aware of the laws of aesthetic structure may not be psychologically free from the need for such illusion. As a result, each motif must be introduced as a *probable* motif in the given situation. But since the laws of plot construction have nothing in common with probability, any introduction of motifs is a compromise between objective reality and literary tradition. We will not mention the utter absurdity of many of the more traditional techniques for introducing motifs. To show the irreconcilability of these absurd traditional techniques with realistic motivation we should have to parody them. See, for example, *Vampuk*, the famous parody of operatic productions which humorously presents a selection of lampoonable traditional operatic situations. This parody is still included in the repertory of The Distorted Mirror.[11]

Accustomed to the techniques of adventure novels, we overlook the absurdity of the fact that the rescue of the hero always occurs five minutes before his seemingly inevitable death; the audience of ancient comedy or the comedy of Molière overlooks the fact that in the last act all the characters turn out to be close relatives (the motif of recognition by the family, as in Molière's *The Miser*. The same situation occurs in Beaumarchais' comedy *The Marriage of Figaro*, but by that time the technique is already dead and so it may

11. The Distorted Mirror was a Petersburg theater which staged parodies. *Vampuk, the African Bride: A Formal Opera in All Respects* was staged there in 1908; the term *Vampuk* was later applied to anything outlandish. *Ed. note.*

be parodied. Nevertheless, the extent to which this motif has survived in dramatic literature is shown by Ostrovsky's *The Guilty Are Without Blame*, where at the end of the play the heroine recognizes the hero as her lost son.) This motif of the recognition of kinship was exceptionally suitable for the ending (kinship reconciles interests, drastically changing the situation), and so became firmly entrenched in the tradition. The explanation that in antiquity the discovery of a lost son and mother was a common event quite misses the mark; it was common only on the stage, in the rigidly conventional nature of literary form.

When traditional means of introducing motifs are debunked during the development of new schools of poetry, of the two kinds of motivation used by the old school (the traditional and the realistic) only the realistic remains after the traditional declines. That is why any literary school which opposes an older aesthetic always produces manifestoes in one form or another about "faithfulness to life" or "adherence to reality." So Boileau wrote in the seventeenth century, defending the young classicism against the traditions of the old French literature; so in the eighteenth century the encyclopedists defended the less elevated genres (the domestic novel and the bourgeois drama) against the old canons; so in the nineteenth century the romantics, in the name of "lifelikeness" and faithfulness to "unadorned nature," rose up against the orthodoxy of the earlier classicism. Succeeding groups even called themselves "Naturalists." In general the nineteenth century abounded in schools whose very names hint at realistic techniques of motivation—"Realism," "Naturalism," "the Nature School," "Populism," and so on. In our time the Symbolists replaced the Realists in the name of some kind of transnaturalism (*de realibus ad realiora*, from the real to the more real) a fact which did not prevent the appearance of Acmeism—which demanded greater attention to the *material* and the *concrete*—and Futurism—which initially rejected aestheticism, desiring at its start to repeat the "original" creative process, and which in its second stage definitely exploited "lower" processes—e.g., realistic motifs.

From school to school we hear the call to "Naturalism." Why, then, has a "completely naturalistic school" not been founded, one which would be the ultimate in Naturalism?—because the name "Realist" is attached to each school (and to none). Naive literary histories use "Realist" as the highest praise of a writer; "Pushkin is a Realist" is a typical historical-literary cliché that does not take into account how the word was used in Pushkin's time. This explains the ever present antagonism of the new school for the old—that is, the exchange of old and obvious conventions for new, less obvious ones within the literary pattern. On the other hand, this also shows that realistic material in itself does not have artistic structure and that the formation of an artistic structure requires that reality be reconstructed according to aesthetic laws. Such laws are always, considered in relation to reality, conventional.

Thus, while the source of realistic motivation is either a naive faith or a demand for illusion, neither prevents the development of literary fantasies. Although folk tales frequently arise among people who believe in the real existence of witches and goblins, their continued existence depends upon some kind of conscious illusion in which a mythological system or fantastic view of the world (i.e., an assumption not really warranted as possible) is present as an illusory hypothesis. On such hypotheses H. G. Wells builds his fantasies— fantasies that are made to seem real not by some mythological system, but by some kind of assumption usually contrary to the laws of nature. (Perelman, in his interesting *Journey to the Planets*, criticizes such fantastic novels because of their unreal assumptions.)

It is curious that in sophisticated literary media influenced by a demand for realistic motivation, fantasies are usually open to a double interpretation. They may be accepted both as real events and as fantasies. In the introduction to Alexey Tolstoy's novel, *The Vampire*, which is an unusually clear example of fantasy, Vladimir Solovyev wrote:

> The real interest and significance of the *fantastic* in literature is con-
> tained in the belief that everything that happens in the world, and
> especially everything that happens in the life of man—except that for
> which the cause is proximate and obvious—still depends on some other
> kind of causation. This other causation is more profound and more
> universal, but to make up for that it is less clear. And this is the
> distinguishing characteristic of the genuinely fantastic; it is never, so to

speak, in full view. Its presence must never compel belief in a mystic interpretation of a vital event; it must rather point, or *hint*, at it. In the really fantastic, the external, formal possibility of a simple explanation of ordinary and commonplace connections among the phenomena always remains. This external explanation, however, finally loses its internal probability. All the individual details must seem ordinary, and only their relation to the whole pattern must point to another cause.

If we remove the touch of idealism the philosopher Solovyev gives these words, they contain a satisfactorily precise formulation of the techniques of the fantastic narrative viewed from the norm of realistic motivation. The tales of Hoffmann, the novels of Mrs. Radcliffe, etc., use the technique. Sleep, delirium, optical or other illusions, and so on, are the usual motifs which permit the possibility of double interpretation. (See Bryusov's collection of stories, *The Axis of the Globe*, in this connection.)

Realistic motivation explains why nonliterary materials—that is, themes having real significance outside the limits of the artistic imagination—are introduced into the work of art. Thus in historical novels historical figures are brought onto the scene with this or that interpretation of the historical events, as in Tolstoy's *War and Peace*. The entire report on the military strategy of the Battle of Borodino and the burning of Moscow reminds one of the debates in specialists' journals. More modern works which depict familiar, everyday life raise questions about the moral, social, political, and other orders; themes whose vitality is outside literature are introduced by a single word. Even in conventional parodies, where we see a deliberate display of techniques, we must ultimately discuss questions of poetics. Thus the so-called "laying bare" of a device (its use without the motivation which traditionally accompanies it) is an indication of the literariness of the literary work, something not unlike the play within a play (that is, a dramatic work in which the spectacle is presented as an element of the story, as in Hamlet's staging of a play or the final scene in Alexandre Dumas' *Kean; ou Désordre et génie*, and so on).

3. *Artistic motivation.* As I said, the use of a motif results from a compromise between realistic illusion and the demands of the

artistic structure. Not everything borrowed from reality is fit for the work of art, as Lermontov noted when he wrote about the journalistic prose of his contemporaries in 1840:

> Whose portraits do they depict?
> Where do they hear their conversations?
> *Yet if they had really happened—*
> *We simply would not want to hear them.*

Boileau said much the same in his play on words, *"le vrai peut quelquefois n'être pas vraisemblable"* ("Sometimes the truth may not seem true"), understanding by *"vrai"* realistic motivation, and by *"vraisemblable"* artistic motivation.

A system of realistic motivation quite often includes a denial of artistic motivation. The usual formula is, "If this had happened in a novel, my hero would have done such and such, but since it really happened, here are the facts. . . ." But the denial of the literary form in itself asserts the laws of artistic composition.

Each realistic motif must somehow be inserted into the structure of the narrative and be illuminated by a particular part of it. The very selection of realistic themes must be justified artistically.

Usually quarrels between new and old literary groups arise over artistic motivation. The old, tradition-oriented group generally denies the artistry of the new literary form. This is shown, for example, in poetic diction, where the use of individual words must be in accord with firmly established literary traditions (tradition, which produces the distinction between prosaic and poetic words, strictly forbids their use together).

I consider the device of *defamiliarization* to be a special instance of artistic motivation. The introduction of nonliterary material into a work, if it is to be aesthetic, must be justified by a new and individual interpretation of the material. The old and habitual must be spoken of as if it were new and unusual. One must speak of the ordinary as if it were unfamiliar.

Techniques of defamiliarizing ordinary things are usually justified because the objects are distorted through the mental processes of a character who is not familiar with them. A well-known example of Leo Tolstoy's use of the technique occurs in *War and Peace* when he describes the council of war at Fils. He introduces a little peasant girl who watches the council and, like a child, interprets what is done and said without understanding it. Tolstoy uses precisely the same method of interpreting human relationships in "Kholstomer," where he presents them through the hypothetical psychology of a horse. (See "Kashtanka," in which Chekhov gives as much of the psychology of a dog as is necessary to defamiliarize the narrative; Korolenko's "The Blind Musician," which interprets the life of the seeing through the psychology of the blind, is of the same type.)

Swift uses these methods of defamiliarization extensively in in *Gulliver's Travels* in order to present a satirical picture of the European social-political order. Gulliver, arriving in the land of the Houyhnhnms (horses endowed with reason), tells his master (a horse) about the customs of the ruling class in human society. Compelled to tell everything with the utmost accuracy, he removes the shell of euphemistic phrases and fictitious traditions which justify such things as war, class strife, parliamentary intrigue, and so on. Stripped of their verbal justification and thereby defamiliarized, these topics emerge in all their horror. Thus criticism of the political system—nonliterary material—is artistically motivated and fully involved in the narrative.

As a specific example of such defamiliarization, I shall cite Pushkin's treatment of the duel in *The Captain's Daughter*. As early as 1830, Pushkin wrote in the *Literary Gazette*:

> People in high society have their own modes of thought, their peculiar prejudices, which are incomprehensible to other classes. How do you explain the duel of two French officers to a peace-loving Eskimo? The delicacy of the officers would seem quite strange to him, and he would hardly be wrong.

Pushkin later used this observation in *The Captain's Daughter*. In the third chapter Mironovaya, the Captain's wife, tells Grinyov why Shvabrin was transferred from the guard to an outlying garrison:

> "Shvabrin was transferred to us five years ago after a murder. God knows what kind of sin he committed. You see, he rode out of the city with a lieutenant, and they took their swords and jabbed at one another, and he began to stab the lieutenant, even though two witnesses were present."

Later, in the fourth chapter, when Shvabrin challenges Grinyov to a duel, the latter turns to a garrison lieutenant and invites him to second the affair:

> "You are pleased to say," he answered, "that you intend to kill Alexey Ivanovich, and you wish me to witness it? Is that it? May I ask?"
>
> "Precisely so."
>
> "Good heavens, Peter Andreyich! What do you think you're doing? You've had words with Alexey Ivanovich? So what? Abuse doesn't stick. He curses you, and you swear back at him. He hits you in the kisser, you hit him on one ear—then two, then three, then you part. And then we see to it that you make up later."

As a result of all this conversation, Grinyov is categorically refused:

> "You may say what you like, but if I am to get mixed up in this business it will be only to go to Ivan Kuzmich and tell him, as my duty requires, that a crime against the public interest is being plotted in this fortress."

In the fifth chapter, Savelyich's comments further defamiliarize the subject of dueling with swords:

> "Not I, but the damned Frenchman, started it all. He taught you to jab people with iron spits and to stamp your feet, as if jabbing and dancing could defend you from a vicious man."

The result of this comic defamiliarization is that the idea of dueling is presented in a fresh, unusual form. Here the defamiliarization is comic, underlined by the diction ("He hits you in the kisser," —the vulgarism "kisser" characterizes the speech of the lieutenant about a rough scuffle; it does not at all describe Grinyov's face. "You hit him on one ear—then two, then three"—counts the number of blows, not ears. Such a clash of words creates the comic effect). But the technique of defamiliarization is, to be sure, not always comic.

4. THE HERO

The usual device for grouping and stringing together motifs is the creation of a character who is the living embodiment of a given collection of motifs. The assignment of this or that motif to a character holds the attention of the reader. The character is a guiding thread which makes it possible to untangle a conglomeration of motifs and permits them to be classified and arranged. Then too, there are devices which aid in untangling the groups of characters and their interrelations. The reader must know how to recognize a character, and the character must attract at least some attention.

A character is recognized by his *characteristics*. By characteristics we mean a system of motifs intimately related to a given person. More narrowly, characteristics are the motifs which define the psychology of the person, his "character."

The simplest characteristic of a person is his name. In uncomplicated story forms it is sometimes enough to give a character a name and no other characteristics (a character in the abstract) in order to define his necessary role in the story. In more complex forms, the behavior of the character must flow from some psychological unity, must be psychologically valid for that character (the psychological motivation of behavior). In such a case the figure is endowed with definite psychological characteristics.

In *direct characterization* the author may characterize the figure directly by a straightforward report; he may have other characters discuss the person in question; or he may have the character tell about himself in, say, a confession of some sort. *Indirect characterization* also occurs frequently; the character in such a case betrays himself in his actions or conduct. Sometimes such actions at the beginning are irrelevant to the story but are necessary for the characterization. Because these actions are unrelated to the story, they seem to be part of the exposition. Thus in K[onstantin] Fedin's story "Anna Timofeyevna," the anecdote about Jakovlev and the nun in the first chapter is given for the purpose of characterization.

The *mask*—the development of concrete motifs in harmony with the psychology of the character—is a special device of either direct or indirect characterization. The description of the external appearance of the hero, his clothes, the furnishings of his apartment (for example, Plyushkin in Gogol)—all these are part of the technique of the mask. *Mask* need not be applied only to the visual appearance of a character; it may take many other forms. The very name of the hero may serve as his mask. In this regard it is interesting to note the comic tradition of using names as masks. From the elementary "Trueman," "Blunt," and "Thorogood" to the more complex "Richard Hardcastle" and "Tony Lumpkin,"[12] almost all comic names contain a hint of characterization. One has only to look at the names of the dramatis personae in Ostrovsky's work.

Two basic kinds of character may be distinguished: the *static character*, who remains exactly the same throughout the development of the story; and the *dynamic character*, whose characteristics change throughout the course of the story. In the latter the elements of characterization enter intimately into the story, and the crisis of the character (often a repentance scene) marks a change in the situation in the story.

On the other hand, the diction of a character, the style of his speech, and the topics he touches upon in conversation may also serve as a mask.

It is not sufficient to differentiate among the characters, to single each out from the rest through specific traits. The writer must arouse the attention of the reader, hold it, and interest him in the fates of the characters. The basic way is to arouse sympathy for the characters, who are usually presented with some emotional coloring. In very primitive forms in which we find good and evil types, the emotional relationship to the character (sympathy or revulsion) is worked out morally. Positive or negative "types" are necessary for the construction of the story. Attracting the reader's sympathy for one character and his repugnance for another calls for his emotional participation in (his "experiencing") the described events; it arouses his personal interest in the fates of the characters.

The character who receives the sharpest and most acute emotional representation is called the *protagonist*. He is the person whom the reader watches with the greatest intensity and attention and who calls forth the reader's compassion, sympathy, joy, and sorrow.

We must not forget that the emotional attitude toward the protagonist is set by his function in the work. An author may arouse

12. Tomashevsky gives as examples such names as Pravdin (Mr. Trueman), Milonov (Mr. Kind), and Skalozub (Mr. Sneerwell). We have supplied names from Lillo's *The London Merchant* and Goldsmith's *She Stoops to Conquer. Ed. note.*

sympathy for a protagonist whose character in real life would provoke revulsion and disgust. The emotional attitude toward the protagonist is a fact of the artistic construction of the tale, and only in primitive forms must it coincide with the orthodox moral and communal codes.

This consideration was frequently overlooked by the journalist-critics of the 1860's, who judged the protagonist from the point of view of the social utility of his character and ideology, separating him from the work of art in which the emotional attitude toward him was established. This occurred, for example, with Ostrovsky's *The Bankrupt*, in which the Russian employer Vasilkov, who opposed the expansion of the nobility, was considered a negative type by our critics among the popular intelligensia. They thought of him as an emerging capitalistic exploiter; in real life they found his type unsympathetic. Such a misinterpretation of a work of art because of its ideology may create a completely insurmountable wall between the reader and the work if the reader begins to evaluate the emotions generated within the work in terms of his everyday personal or political feelings. To read, one must be innocent, must catch the signs the author gives. The greater the talent of the author, the more difficult it is to resist the emotional directives, the more convincing the work. Because literature is so persuasive, we naturally assume that it should perform the duties of a teacher and have the authority of a preacher.

The protagonist is by no means an essential part of the story. The story, as a system of motifs, may dispense entirely with him and his characteristics. The protagonist, rather, is the result of the formation of the story material into a plot. On the one hand, he is a means of stringing motifs together; and on the other, he embodies the motivation which connects the motifs. This is clear in an elementary narrative form like the anecdote, which, generally speaking, is a quite unstable, vague, and small form of story structure and is in many cases the combination of just two main motifs. (The other motifs are necessary for giving the circumstances, introducing the material, and so on.) The combination of the motifs creates a special effect of double meaning, of contrast, which is described by the French terms *bon mot* (witty remark) and *pointe* (literally, "sharpness," the idea of the Italian *concetti*; "epigram" is somewhat similar).

Let us take an anecdote constructed on two motifs which combine into a single formation (the pun). An illiterate preacher arrived in a certain village where the parishoners awaited his sermon. He began thus, "You know what I will speak about?"

"No, we don't know."

"Then why should I talk to you about what you don't know?" The sermon was not given. The anecdote has a sequel which further emphasizes the double meaning of "to know." The next time the parishoners were asked the same question, they answered, "We know."

"Then if you know before I give my sermon, I have nothing to say to you."

In some versions there is a continuation. Part of the congregation answers "We know," and part "We don't know." This time the preacher's answer is, "Will those who do know kindly tell those who don't know."

This anecdote is constructed solely on the double meaning of one word, and its effectiveness does not depend upon the circumstances in which the dialogue might occur. But in its concrete form, the dialogue always fixes upon some kind of protagonist (usually a preacher). The cunning yet incompetent preacher and his duped flock are the contingent elements of the story; but, nevertheless, some character is necessary to hold the anecdote together.

Here is an example of a more complicated anecdote from English folklore. The characters are an Englishman and an Irishman (in popular English anecdotes the Irishman is a special type who thinks slowly and not always successfully). They are on the road to London and read the following inscription at an intersection: "This is the road to London. Whoever cannot read may ask the blacksmith who lives beyond the bend in the road." The Englishman bursts into laughter, but the Irishman remains silent. That evening they arrive in London and arrange to spend the night in a hotel. During the night the Englishman is awakened by the uncontrolled laughter of the Irishman. "What's the matter?" "Now I understand why you laughed when you read the inscription by the road." "Well?" "You

see, the blacksmith might not be at home." Here are clashing motifs
—the Irishman's unique interpretation and the obvious humor of
the inscription, which assumes, as did the author of the inscription,
that an illiterate person might actually read it.

But such anecdotes are usually developed by attaching the motifs
to a well-known character whose personality reflects his nationality
(similarly anecdotes about Gascons thrive in France, and we have
numerous native and provincial anecdotal heroes). Or the hero's
name may readily characterize him because he is a well-known
historical person (in France, the Duke Gaston Roquelaure; in
Germany, Till Eulenspiegel; in Russia, the jester Balakirev). Likewise, anecdotes are attributed to various historical persons
(Napoleon, Diogenes, Pushkin, etc.). Ultimately the gradual stringing together of motifs on the the thread provided by the character or
"name" creates an anecdotal type. The process is analogous to the
origin of the characters in Italian comedy (Harlequin, Piero,
Pantaloon).

5. THE VITALITY OF PLOT DEVICES

Although the general devices of plot construction of all lands and
all peoples are significantly similar, and although it is possible to
speak about the unique logic of plot construction, it is nevertheless
true that specific devices, their combinations, their use, and their
functions have changed greatly in the course of literary history. Each
literary period, each school, is characterized by the system of
devices which are present in the common style (in the broad sense
of "style") of its literary genres and preferences.

In this respect we must distinguish between *conventional* and *free*
devices. Conventional devices are devices required by a given genre
and a given period; the French classicism of the seventeenth century,
with its dramatic unities and petty regulation of various genre forms,
produced the strictest system of conventional devices. Conventional
devices are the trade-marks of the works produced by a school that
accepts that particular convention. In any typical seventeenth-
century tragedy the place of action remains unchanged and the time
is limited to twenty-four hours. All comedies end in marriage, and
all tragedies in the deaths of the principal characters. Any convention

establishes its own set of devices. Everything in literature—from the choice of thematic materials, the various motifs and their use together, to systematic pronouncements about language, diction, etc.—may be made into a conventional device. The use of one word and the proscription of another, and so on, may be subject to regulation. Conventional devices originate because they are convenient technically; their repetition becomes traditional, and, falling into the area of normative poetics, they are codified as compulsory rules. But no convention can exhaust all possibilities and foresee all the devices necessary for the creation of an entire work, so that along with the conventional devices there are always free devices—devices peculiar to individual writers, works, genres, movements, etc.

Conventional devices usually destroy themselves. One value of literature is its novelty and originality. In the struggle for regeneration, the orthodox, the traditional, the stereotyped devices are most attacked, and the obligatory becomes the prohibited. The creation of new traditions and techniques does not, however, prevent the revival of prohibited devices after the passing of two or three literary generations.

Consequently, since our evaluation of and attention to literary methods are reactions to the various techniques, we may classify these as *perceptible* (obvious) and *imperceptible* (unobvious).

Devices are perceptible for perhaps two reasons: their excessive age or their excessive newness. Abandoned, old, archaic devices are felt as intrusive remnants, as having lost their own vitality and enduring by a strong inertial force, like a dead body among living beings. On the other hand, new devices strike their own peculiar, unaccustomed note if they are taken from a previously forbidden repertory (vulgarisms in serious poetry, for example). We must keep our appreciation of perceptible and imperceptible devices in a historical perspective. The language of Pushkin seems smooth to us, and we almost miss its peculiarities; yet he startled his contemporaries by the strangeness of his ludicrous Slavisms and his colloquial diction. They thought his work rough and uneven. Only contemporaries may judge the perceptibility of a given device. We no longer notice that structural roughness of the works of the Symbolists which had so shocked the literary "old believers" before

1908; but, on the other hand, we tend to find the early works of Balmont and Bryusov trite and prosaic.

Two literary styles may be distinguished in terms of the perceptibility of the devices. The first, characteristic of writers of the nineteenth century, is distinguished by its attempt to conceal the device; all of its motivation systems are designed to make the literary devices seem imperceptible, to make them seem as natural as possible—that is, to develop the literary material so that its development is unperceived. But this is only one style, and not a general aesthetic rule. It is opposed to another style, an unrealistic style, which does not bother about concealing the devices and which frequently tries to make them obvious, as when a writer interrupts a speech he is reporting to say that he did not hear how it ended, only to go on and report what he has no realistic way of knowing. In such a case, the author has called attention to the device or—as they say—the technique is "laid bare." Pushkin, in the fourth chapter of *Evgeny Onegin*, writes:

> And here already sparkle the snows
> And they spread among silver fields—
> (The reader waits for a rhyme like rose;
> Let him take quickly what this poem yields).

Here we have a clear and deliberate laying bare of the technique of rhyme.

In the early stages of Futurism (in the works of Khlebnikov) and in contemporary literature, the laying bare of techniques had become traditional (many of the tales of Kaverin contain examples of the laying bare of devices of plot structure).

Among works containing such devices, we must distinguish those which lay bare extraneous devices—either traditional devices or those belonging to another writer. If the laying bare of extraneous literary devices is humorous, we have parody. The functions of parody are many, but its usual function is to ridicule an opposing literary group, blasting its aesthetic system and exposing it.

Parodies are quite widespread; they were traditional in dramatic literature, when any more or less outstanding work called for an immediate parody. The background from which a parody takes off is always another literary work (or a whole group of works). A significant number of parodies may be found among the tales of Chekhov.

Some parodies, not primarily satiric, are developed freely for the sole purpose of showing off the techniques. Thus the followers of Laurence Sterne at the start of the nineteenth century formed their own school, which had developed out of parody, into a school which pursued parody as an art in its own right. In contemporary literature, Sterne's techniques have been revived and widely disseminated (the transposition of chapters, excessive and casual digressions, the slowing of the action, and so on, are typical).

Devices are laid bare because a perceptible device is permissible only when it is made creatively outstanding. When a device is noticed despite the author's attempt to conceal it, it produces a detrimentally comic effect. To prevent this, the author deliberately lays bare the device.[13]

Thus devices are born, live, grow old, and die. To the extent that their use becomes automatic, they lose their efficacy and cease to be included on the list of acceptable techniques. Renovated devices with new functions and new meanings are required to prevent techniques from becoming mechanical. Such renovation is like the use of a quotation from an old author in a new application and with a new meaning.

[The "Thematics" continues with a discussion of the concept of literary genres, followed by discussions of the dramatic, lyric, and fictional genres.]

Boris Tomashevsky, "Tematika," *Teoriya literatury* [*Theory of Literature*] (Leningrad, 1925).

13. In "Pure and Impure Poetry" Robert Penn Warren's argument is quite similar, although it is based upon what Tomashevsky would call "realistic motivation" rather than convention. Warren argues that the content of even lyric poetry requires some alloy of "impurity" or "irony" to keep the reader from snickering. *Ed. note.*

BORIS EICHENBAUM

In the following selection, three asterisks (* * *) are used to indicate that a portion of the original has been omitted.

The Theory of the "Formal Method"

"The Theory of the 'Formal Method'" [1] *provides an admirable overview of the work of the Russian Formalists.* Boris Eichenbaum joined the Opoyaz group *shortly after its formation in 1914 and quickly became one of its most prolific and influential members. His essay "How Gogol's 'Greatcoat' Was Made" was an important contribution to the first collection of Formalist essays,* Poetics: Studies in the Theory of Poetic Language. [2] *Articles and books on a variety of subjects followed, ranging from "The Melody of Verse" and a full-length study of the work of the poet Anna Akhmatova, through studies of Lermontov, Leo Tolstoy, and O. Henry, to general speculations on literature (especially the novel) and a journal of essays, criticism, and stories which he wrote and edited himself.* [3]

By 1926 Eichenbaum and his fellow Formalists found themselves under heavy attack. The attack had started in 1923, after the Formalists had begun to attract a number of young disciples, in Leo Trotsky's Literature and the Revolution, *which devoted an entire chapter to "The Formalist School."* [4] *Trotsky's attack was not devastating. Although sharply worded and largely uninformed of the rapidly growing breadth and depth of Formalist study, it did not demand the dissolution of the movement. Trotsky's main point, briefly, was that the Formalist approach to literature was grossly incomplete. The exclusive concentration upon the literariness of literature and the autonomy of art (or, in later phases of Formalism, upon the autonomy of literature as a field of investigation) ignored what from the Marxist point of view was most*

1. Eichenbaum's "Teoriya 'formalnovo metoda,'" was first published in Ukranian in 1926. The text used here is the Russian text in *Literatura: Teoriya, kritika, polemika* [*Literature: Theory, Criticism, Polemics*] (Leningrad, 1927).

2. *Poetika: Sborniki po teorii poeticheskovo yazyka* (Petrograd, 1919). Included were essays by Brik, Jakubinsky, and Shklovsky.

3. Victor Erlich, *Russian Formalism: History-Doctrine* (Vol. IV of *Slavistic Printings and Reprintings*, ed. Cornelis H. Van Schooneveld; 'S-Gravenhage: Mouton & Co., 1955), pp. 253–254, gives a bibliography of Eichenbaum's Formalist publications.

4. Leo Trotsky, *Literature and the Revolution* (New York: Russell & Russell, 1957), Chap. V.

crucial—the social causes and effects of art. Trotsky saw Formalism as concerned only with the technical aspects of literature, as a mechanical enumeration of literary devices. He admitted its value as a technical study; he found it valueless and vicious as a complete system of literary study.

The next stage in the attack came in 1924, in the journal The Press and the Revolution. *An article by Anatoly Lunacharsky,[5] the first Soviet Commissar of Education, took up where Trotsky left off and, by going further, substantially altered the nature of the charge against the Formalists. The key term in the bill of particulars was no longer "narrow," but "decadent." The specific attack was that Formalism encouraged art for the sake of art and promoted aesthetic sterility. But the still unsettled nature of the official attitude is best shown by the fact that the same issue of* The Press and the Revolution *contained a defense of Formalism in which Eichenbaum answered Trotsky by arguing that Formalism and Marxism were mutually irrelevant. The former explained literature from the inside, the latter from the outside; because each had a different object of study, there could be no real conflict between them.*

A number of interesting attempts to reconcile the two approaches followed, the most promising being the line pursued by such theorists as Alexander Zeitlin, whose general line of argument was that the Marxist sociological analyses of literature could not proceed effectively until theorists knew the nature of the thing they were studying—in short, the internal descriptive work of the Formalists would have to precede any development of a broader literary theory.

The original Formalists themselves, in particular Shklovsky and Eichenbaum, also attempted a compromise. Shklovsky's compromise was a confused and partial recantation, Eichenbaum's a deliberate attempt to broaden a method which he had begun to find too constraining.[6] Internally, Formalism faced much the same problem the New Criticism faced after its initial success. Having begun with specific and precise problems, it found that the specific led

5. *Pechat i revolyutsiya,* No. 5.

6. See especially Shklovsky's *Tretya fabrika* [*Third Factory*] (Moscow, 1926) and his "*Voyna i mir Lva Tolstovo* (Formalno-sotsiologicheskoye issledovaniye)" ["*War and Peace* of Leo Tolstoy (A Formalistic-Sociological Study)"], *Novy lef* [*New Left*], No. 1 (1928), and the short-lived journal Eichenbaum wrote and edited himself, *Moy vremennik* [*My Times*] (1929).

only to the general. Unfortunately, the Formalist movement was ended before it fully explored the problems its method posed.

Such, then, was the condition of Formalism at the time of Eichenbaum's summary of the movement. Or perhaps "summary" is not the precise word, for in many respects "The Theory of the 'Formal Method'" reads more like an apologia—a defense carefully calculated to appeal to a hostile audience without distortion of the basic doctrines involved. This perhaps explains Eichenbaum's insistence upon the scientific nature of the Formal method, an insistence that is likely to annoy Western readers. Eichenbaum could not in conscience claim that Formalism was in any sense Marxist in orientation; the simplest and most logical recourse was to insist upon, perhaps even to exaggerate, the notion that the Formalists were engaged merely in a nonideological study of data, that whatever hypotheses they used developed out of the observation of facts and were modified by those facts. The strategy, if we correctly surmise Eichenbaum's aim, was to argue that Formalism was scientific, and thus compatible with Marxism. On the other hand, it should not be forgotten that Eichenbaum's strategy is at most exaggeration, not falsification; the work of the Formalists is characterized by a desire for accuracy and concreteness that it did not always attain.

Eichenbaum is also guilty of another exaggeration. The reader of "The Theory of the 'Formal Method'" is led to sense a logic of consistent progression within the history of the movement, a consistency improbable for a group of diverse talents dealing with a huge and complex subject. Time and again Eichenbaum varies the formula, "Having disposed of that, we turned to this," as if a dozen or so of Russia's most brilliant literary theoreticians brainstormed through one problem, neatly published a definitive solution, then moved on to something else. Actually, the Formalists no more "solved" the problems involved in such concepts as defamiliarization or motivation than the New Critics solved the problems of irony or metaphor. The leading practitioners rather reached a point of diminishing returns and so began to invest their time in other, but closely related, areas. Once these two types of exaggeration (the scientism of the Formalists and the orderly progress of their research) are discounted, Eichenbaum's essay takes its place as an adequate and accurate summary of the Russian Formalist movement.

The subtitles in this selection have been editorially supplied.

The worst, in my opinion, are those who describe science as if it were settled.

[*Le pire, à mon avis, est celui qui représente la science comme faite.*]—
A. DE CANDOLLE

The so-called "formal method" grew out of a struggle for a science of literature that would be both independent and factual; it is not the outgrowth of a particular methodology. The notion of a "method" has been so exaggerated that it now suggests too much. In principle the question for the Formalist[7] is not how to study literature, but what the subject matter of literary study actually is. We neither discuss methodology nor quarrel about it. We speak and may speak only about theoretical principles suggested to us not by this or that ready-made methodology, but by the examination of specific material in its specific context. The Formalists' works in literary theory and literary history show this clearly enough, but during the past ten years so many new questions and old misunderstandings have accumulated that I feel it advisable to try to summarize some of our work—not as a dogmatic system but as a historical summation. I wish to show how the work of the Formalists began, how it evolved, and what it evolved into.

The evolutionary character of the development of the formal method is important to an understanding of its history; our opponents and many of our followers overlook it. We are surrounded by eclectics and late-comers who would turn the formal method into some kind of inflexible "formalistic" system in order to provide themselves with a working vocabulary, a program, and a name. A program is a very handy thing for critics, but not at all characteristic of our method. Our scientific approach has had no such prefabricated program or doctrine, and has none. In our studies we value a theory only as a working hypothesis to help us discover and interpret facts; that is, we determine the validity of the facts and use them as the material of our research. We are not concerned with definitions, for which the late-comers thirst; nor do we build general theories, which so

7. By "Formalists" I mean in this essay only that group of theoreticians who made up the Society for the Study of Poetic Language (the *Opoyaz*) and who began to publish their studies in 1916. [Actually, Eichenbaum also includes as Formalists members of the Moscow Linguistic Circle; see above, p. xiv, note 9.]

delight eclectics. We posit specific principles and adhere to them insofar as the material justifies them. If the material demands their refinement or change, we change or refine them. In this sense we are quite free from our own theories—as science must be free to the extent that theory and conviction are distinct. There is no ready-made science; science lives not by settling on truth, but by over-coming error.

This essay is not intended to argue our position. The initial period of scientific struggle and journalistic polemics is past. Such attacks as that in *The Press and the Revolution*[8] (with which I was honored) can be answered only by new scientific works. My chief purpose here is to show how the formal method, by gradually evolving and broadening its field of research, spread beyond the usual "methodological" limits and became a special science of literature, a specific ordering of facts. Within the limits of this science, the most diverse methods may develop, if only because we focus on the empirical study of the material. Such study was, essentially, the aim of the Formalists from the very beginning, and precisely that was the significance of our quarrel with the old traditions. The name "formal method," bestowed upon the move-ment and now firmly attached to it, may be tentatively understood as a historical term; it should not be taken as an accurate description of our work. Neither "Formalism" as an aesthetic theory nor "methodology" as a finished scientific system characterizes us; we are characterized only by the attempt to create an independent science of literature which studies specifically literary material. We ask only for recognition of the theoretical and historical facts of literary art as such.

1. THE ORIGINS OF FORMALISM

Representatives of the formal method were frequently reproached by various groups for their lack of clarity or for the inadequacy of their principles—for indifference to general questions of aesthetics, sociology, psychology, and so on. These reproofs, despite their varying merit, are alike in that they correctly grasp that the chief characteristic of the Formalists is indeed their deliberate isolation both from "aesthetics from above" and from all ready-made or

8. See above, p. 100. *Ed. note.*

self-styled general theories. This isolation (particularly from aesthetics) is more or less typical of all contemporary studies of art. Dismissing a whole group of general problems (problems of beauty, the aims of art, etc.), the contemporary study of art concentrates on the concrete problems of aesthetics [*Kunstwissenschaft*]. Without reference to socio-aesthetic premises, it raises questions about the idea of artistic "form" and its evolution. It thereby raises a series of more specific theoretical and historical questions. Such familiar slogans as Wölfflin's "history of art without names" [*Kunstgeschichte ohne Nahmen*][9] characterized experiments in the empirical analysis of style and technique (like Voll's "experiment in the comparative study of paintings"). In Germany especially the study of the theory and history of the visual arts, which had had there an extremely rich history of tradition and experiment, occupied a central position in art studies and began to influence the general theory of art and its separate disciplines—in particular, the study of literature.[10] In Russia, apparently for local historical reasons, literary studies occupied a place analogous to that of the visual arts in Germany.

The formal method has attracted general attention and become controversial not, of course, because of its distinctive methodology, but rather because of its characteristic attitude toward the understanding and the study of technique. The Formalists advocated principles which violated solidly entrenched traditional notions, notions which had appeared to be "axiomatic" not only in the study of literature, but in the study of art generally. Because they adhered to their principles so strictly, they narrowed the distance between particular problems of literary theory and general problems of aesthetics. The ideas and principles of the Formalists, for all their concreteness, were pointedly directed towards a general theory of aesthetics. Our creation of a radically unconventional poetics, therefore, implied more than a simple reassessment of particular problems; it had an impact on the study of art generally. It had its impact

9. See Hinrich Wölfflin's *Kunstgeschichtliche Grundbegriffe* (Munich, 1915). Wölfflin was one of the originators of the stylistic analysis of art. *Ed. note.*

10. R[udolph] Unger notes the strong influence of the work of Wölfflin on such representatives of the "aesthetic" trend in German historical-literary study as O[skar] Walzel and F[ritz] Strich. See his article, "Moderne Strömungen in der deutschen Literaturwissenschaft," *Die Literatur*, II (November 1923). Cf. also Walzel's *Gehalt und Gestalt im Kunstwerk des Dichters* (Berlin, 1923).

because of a series of historical developments, the most important of which were the crisis in philosophical aesthetics and the startling innovations in art (in Russia most abrupt and most clearly defined in poetry). Aesthetics seemed barren and art deliberately denuded— in an entirely primitive condition. Hence, Formalism and Futurism seemed bound together by history.

But the general historical significance of the appearance of Formalism comprises a special theme; I must speak of something else here because I intend to show how the principles and problems of the formal method evolved and how the Formalists came to their present position.

Before the appearance of the Formalists, academic research, quite ignorant of theoretical problems, made use of antiquated aesthetic, psychological, and historical "axioms" and had so lost sight of its proper subject that its very existence as a science had become illusory. There was almost no struggle between the Formalists and the Academicians, not because the Formalists had broken in the door (there were no doors), but because we found an open passageway instead of a fortress. The theoretical heritage which Potebnya and Veselovsky left to their disciples seemed to lay like dead capital —a treasure which they were afraid to touch, the brilliance of which they had allowed to fade. In fact, authority and influence had gradually passed from academic scholarship to the "scholarship" of the journals, to the work of the Symbolist critics and theoreticians. Actually, between 1907 and 1912 the books and essays of Vyacheslav Ivanov, Bryusov, Merezhkovsky, Chukovsky, and others, were much more influential than the scholarly studies and dissertations of the university professors. This journalistic "scholarship," with all its subjectivity and tendentiousness, was supported by the theoretical principles and slogans of the new artistic movements and their propagandists. Such books as Bely's *Simvolizm* (1910) naturally meant much more to the younger generation than the monographs on the history of literature which sprang up from no set of principles and which showed that the authors completely lacked both a scientific temperament and a scientific point of view.

The historical battle between the two generations [the Symbolists and the Formalists]—a battle which was fought over principles and was extraordinarily intense—was therefore resolved in the journals, and the battle line was drawn over Symbolist theory and Impression-istic criticism rather than over any work being done by the Academicians. We entered the fight against the Symbolists in order to wrest poetics from their hands—to free it from its ties with their subjective philosophical and aesthetic theories and to direct it toward the scientific investigation of facts. We were raised on their works, and we saw their errors with the greatest clarity. At this time, the struggle became even more urgent because the Futurists (Khlebnikov, Kruchenykh, and Mayakovsky), who were on the rise, opposed the Symbolist poetics and supported the Formalists.

The original group of Formalists was united by the idea of liberating poetic diction from the fetters of the intellectualism and moralism which more and more obsessed the Symbolists. The dissension among the Symbolist theoreticians (1910–1911) and the appearance of the Acmeists [11] prepared the way for our decisive rebellion. We knew that all compromises would have to be avoided, that history demanded of us a really revolutionary attitude—a categorical thesis, merciless irony, and bold rejections of whatever could not be reconciled with our position. We had to oppose the subjective aesthetic principles espoused by the Symbolists with an objective consideration of the facts. Hence our Formalist movement was characterized by a new passion for scientific positivism—a rejection of philosophical assumptions, of psychological and aesthetic interpretations, etc. Art, considered apart from philosophical aesthetics and ideological theories, dictated its own position on things. We had to turn to facts and, abandoning general systems and problems, to begin "in the middle," with the facts which art forced upon us. Art demanded that we approach it closely; science, that we deal with the specific.

2. THE SCIENCE OF LITERATURE:
THE INDEPENDENT VALUE OF POETIC SOUND

The establishment of a specific and factual literary science was basic to the organization of the formal method. All of our efforts

11. The Acmeists, like the Futurists, rebelled against the principles and practices of the Symbolists. But unlike the Futurists, they attempted a highly controlled, polished style of poetry. The best-known Acmeists were Anna Akhmatova and Osip Mandelstam. The movement did not survive World War I. *Ed. note.*

were directed toward disposing of the earlier position which, according to Alexander Veselovsky, made of literature an abandoned thing [a *res nullius*]. This is why the position of the Formalists could not be reconciled with other approaches and was so unacceptable to the eclectics. In rejecting these other approaches, the Formalists actually rejected and still reject not the methods, but rather the irresponsible mixing of various disciplines and their problems. The basis of our position was and is that the object of literary science, as such, must be the study of those specifics which distinguish it from any other material. (The secondary, incidental features of such material, however, may reasonably and rightly be used in a subordinate way by other scientific disciplines.) Roman Jakobson formulated this view with perfect clarity:

> The object of the science of literature is not literature, but literariness— that is, that which makes a given work a work of literature. Until now literary historians have preferred to act like the policeman who, intending to arrest a certain person, would, at any opportunity, seize any and all persons who chanced into the apartment, as well as those who passed along the street. The literary historians used everything— anthropology, psychology, politics, philosophy. Instead of a science of literature, they created a conglomeration of homespun disciplines. They seemed to have forgotten that their essays strayed into related disciplines—the history of philosophy, the history of culture, of psychology, etc.—and that these could rightly use literary masterpieces only as defective, secondary documents.[12]

To apply and strengthen this principle of specificity and to avoid speculative aesthetics, we had to compare literary facts with other kinds of facts, extracting from a limitless number of important orders of fact that order which would pertain to literature and would distinguish it from the others by its function. This was the method Leo Jakubinsky followed in his essays in the first *Opoyaz* collection, in which he worked out the contrast between poetic and practical language that served as the basic principle of the Formalists' work on key problems of poetics. As a result, the Formalists did not look,

12. Roman Jakobson, *Noveyshaya russkaya poeziya* [*Modern Russian Poetry*] (Prague, 1921) p. 11. [Jakobson, it should be stressed, is not arguing that literature is unrelated to history, psychology, etc. He is, rather, insisting that the study of literature, if it is to be a distinct discipline, must have its own particular subject.]

as literary students usually had, toward history, culture, sociology, psychology, or aesthetics, etc., but toward linguistics, a science bordering on poetics and sharing material with it, but approaching it from a different perspective and with different problems. Linguistics, for its part, was also interested in the formal method in that what was discovered by comparing poetic and practical language could be studied as a purely linguistic problem, as part of the general phenomena of language. The relationship between linguistics and the formal method was somewhat analogous to that relation of mutual use and delimitation that exists, for example, between physics and chemistry. Against this background, the problems posed earlier by Potebnya and taken for granted by his followers were reviewed and reinterpreted.

Leo Jakubinsky's first essay, "On the Sounds of Poetic Language," [13] compared practical and poetic language and formulated the difference between them:

> The phenomena of language must be classified from the point of view of the speaker's particular purpose as he forms his own linguistic pattern. If the pattern is formed for the purely practical purpose of communication, then we are dealing with a system of *practical language* (the language of thought) in which the linguistic pattern (sounds, morphological features, etc.) have no independent value and are merely a *means* of communication. But other linguistic systems, systems in which the practical purpose is in the background (although perhaps not entirely hidden) are conceivable; they exist, and their linguistic patterns acquire *independent value*.

The establishment of this distinction was important both for the construction of a poetics and for understanding the Futurist's preference for "nonsense language" as revealing the furthest extension of the sheer "independent" value of words, the kind of value partially observed in the language of children, in the glossolalia of religious sects, and so on. The Futurist experiments in nonsense language were of prime significance as a demonstration against Symbolism which, in its theories, went no further than to use the idea of "instrumentation" to indicate the accompaniment of meaning by sound and so to de-emphasize the role of sound in

13. Leo Jakubinsky, "O zvukakh poeticheskovo yazyka," *Sborniki*, I (1916).

poetic language. The problem of sound in verse was especially crucial because it was on this point that the Formalists and Futurists united to confront the theorists of Symbolism. Naturally, the Formalists gave battle at first on just that issue; the question of sound had to be disposed of first if we were to oppose the aesthetic and philosophical tendencies of the Symbolists with a system of precise observations and to reach the underlying scientific conclusions. This accounts for the content of the first volume of *Opoyaz*, a content devoted entirely to the problem of sound and nonsense language.

Victor Shklovsky, along with Jakubinsky, in "On Poetry and Nonsense Language,"[14] cited a variety of examples which showed that "even words without meaning are necessary." He showed such meaninglessness to be both a widespread linguistic fact and a phenomenon characteristic of poetry. "The poet does not decide to use the meaningless word; usually "nonsense" is disguised as some kind of frequently delusive, deceptive content. Poets are forced to acknowledge that they themselves do not understand the content of their own verses." Shklovsky's essay, moreover, transfers the question from the area of pure sound, from the acoustical level (which provided the basis for impressionistic interpretations of the relation between sound and the description of objects or the emotion represented) to the level of pronunciation and articulation. "In the enjoyment of a meaningless 'nonsense word,' the articulatory aspect of speech is undoubtedly important. Perhaps generally a great part of the delight of poetry consists in pronunciation, in the independent dance of the organs of speech." The question of meaningless language thus became a serious scientific concern, the solution of which would help to clarify many problems of poetic language in general. Shklovsky also formulated the general question:

> If we add to our demand of the word as such that it serve to clarify understanding, that it be generally meaningful, then of course "meaningless" language, as a relatively superficial language, falls by the wayside. But it does not fall alone; a consideration of the facts forces one to wonder whether words always have a meaning, not only in meaningless speech, but also in simple poetic speech—or whether this notion is only a fiction resulting from our inattention.

14. Victor Shklovsky, "O poezii i zaumnom yazyke," *Sborniki*, I (1916).

The natural conclusion of these observations and principles was that poetic language is not only a language of images, that sounds in verse are not at all merely elements of a superficial euphony, and that they do not play a mere "accompaniment" to meaning, but rather that they have an independent significance. The purpose of this work was to force a revision of Potebnya's general theory, which had been built on the conviction that poetry is "thought in images."[15] Potebnya's analysis of poetry, the analysis which the Symbolists had adopted, treated the sound of verse as "expressive" of something behind it. Sound was merely onomatopoetic, merely "aural description." The works of Andrey Bely (who discovered the complete sound picture that champagne makes when poured from a bottle into a glass in two lines from Pushkin, and who also discovered the "noisomeness of a hangover" in Blok's repetition of the consonantal cluster *rdt*) were quite typical.[16] Such attempts to "explain" alliteration, bordering on parody, required a rebuff and an attempt to produce concrete evidence showing that sounds in verse exist apart from any connection with imagery, that they have an independent oral function.

Leo Jakubinsky, in his essays, provided linguistic support for [our arguments in favor of] the independent value of sound in verse. Osip Brik's essay on "Sound Repetitions"[17] illustrated the same point with quotations from Pushkin and Lermontov arranged to present a variety of models. Brik doubted the correctness of the common opinion that poetic language is a language of "images":

No matter how one looks at the interrelationship of image and sound, there is undoubtedly only one conclusion possible—the sounds, the harmonies, are not only euphonious accessories to meaning; they are also the result of an independent poetic purpose. The superficial devices of euphony do not completely account for the instrumentation of poetic speech. Such instrumentation represents on the whole an intricate product of the interaction of the general laws of harmony. Rhyme,

15. See above, pp. 5–7. *Ed. note.*
16. See the essay, "A. Bely," *Skifi [Scythians]* (1917), and *Vetv [Branch]* (1917): also my essay, "O zvukakh v stikhe" ["On Sound in Verse"], reprinted in *Skvoz literaturu [Through Literature]* (Leningrad, 1924).
17. Osip Brik, "Zvukovye povtory," *Sborniki*, II (1917).

alliteration, etc., are only obvious manifestations, particular cases, of the basic laws of euphony.

In opposing the work of Bely, Brik, in the same essay, made no comment at all on the meaning of this or that use of alliteration, but merely affirmed that repetition in verse is analogous to tautology in folklore—that is, that repetition itself plays something of an aesthetic role: "Obviously we have here diverse forms of one general principle, the principle of simple combination, by which either the sounds of the words or their meanings, or now one and now the other, serve as the material of the combination." Such an extension of one device to cover the various forms of poetic material is quite characteristic of the work of the Formalists during their initial period. After the presentation of Brik's essay the question of sound in verse lost something of its urgency, and the Formalists turned to questions of poetics in general.

3. CONTENT AND CORRESPONDENT FORM
VERSUS TECHNIQUE AS CONTENT

The Formalists began their work with the question of the sounds of verse—at that time the most controversial and most basic question. Behind this particular question of poetics stood more general theses which had to be formulated. The distinction between systems of poetic and practical language, which defined the work of the Formalists from the very beginning, was bound to result in the formulation of a whole group of basic questions. The idea of poetry as "thought by means of images" and the resulting formula, "Poetry = Imagery," clearly did not coincide with our observations and contradicted our tentative general principles.[18] Rhythm, sound, syntax—all of these seemed secondary from such a point of view; they seemed uncharacteristic of poetry and necessarily extraneous

18. This refusal to establish any one element—except rhythm, which is unavoidable in temporal arts such as literature—as the one essential of poetry is perhaps the theoretical feature that distinguished the Formalists from their later counterparts in Britain and America. By refusing to single out some such quality as irony or ambiguity, in the manner of Cleanth Brooks or William Empson, the Formalists achieved a literary theory that was at once broad and flexible. *Ed. note.*

to it. The Symbolists accepted Potebnya's general theory because it justified the supremacy of the image-symbol; yet they could not rid themselves of the notorious theory of the "harmony of form and content" even though it clearly contradicted their bent for formal experimentation and discredited it by making it seem mere "aestheticism." The Formalists, when they abandoned Potebnya's point of view, also freed themselves from the traditional correlation of "form and content" and from the traditional idea of form as an envelope, a vessel into which one pours a liquid (the content). The facts of art demonstrate that art's uniqueness consists not in the "parts" which enter into it but in their original *use*. Thus the notion of form was changed; the new notion of form required no companion idea, no correlative.

Even before the formation of the *Opoyaz* in 1914, at the time of the public performances of the Futurists, Shklovsky had published a monograph, *The Resurrection of the Word*,[19] in which he took exception partly to the concepts set forth by Potebnya and partly to those of Veselovsky (the question of imagery was not then of major significance) to advance the principle of perceptible form as the specific sign of artistic awareness:

> We do not experience the commonplace, we do not see it; rather, we recognize it. We do not see the walls of our room; and it is very difficult for us to see errors in proofreading, especially if the material is written in a language we know well, because we cannot force ourselves to see, to read, and not to "recognize" the familiar word. If we have to define specifically "poetic" perception and artistic perception in general, then we suggest this definition: "Artistic" perception is that perception in which we experience form—perhaps not form alone, but certainly form.[20]

Perception here is clearly not to be understood as a simple psychological concept (the perception peculiar to this or that person), but, since art does not exist outside of perception, as an element in art itself. The notion of "form" here acquires new meaning; it is no longer an envelope, but a complete thing, something concrete, dynamic, self-contained, and without a correlative of any kind.

19. Victor Shklovsky, *Voskresheniye slova* (Petersburg, 1914).
20. See above, p. 11 ff. *Ed. note.*

Here we made a decisive break with the Symbolist principle that some sort of "content" is to shine through the "form." And we broke with "aestheticism"—the preference for certain elements of form consciously isolated from "content."

But these general acknowledgements that there are differences between poetic and practical language and that the specific quality of art is shown in its particular use of the material were not adequate when we tried to deal with specific works. We had to find more specific formulations of the principle of perceptible form so that they could make possible the analysis of form itself—the analysis of form understood as content. We had to show that the perception of form results from special artistic techniques which force the reader to experience the form. Shklovsky's "Art as Technique," presenting its own manifesto of the Formalist method, offered a perspective for the concrete analysis of form. Here was a really clear departure from Potebnya and Potebnyaism and, at the same time, from the theoretical principles of Symbolism. The essay began with objections to Potebnya's basic view of imagery and its relation to content. Shklovsky indicates, among other things, that images are almost always static:

> The more you understand an age, the more convinced you become that the images a given poet used and which you thought his own were taken almost unchanged from another poet. The works of poets are classified or grouped according to the new techniques they discover and share, and according to their arrangement and development of the resources of language; poets are much more concerned with arranging images than creating them. Images are given to poets; the ability to remember them is far more important than the ability to create them. Imagistic thought does not, in any case, include all aspects of art or even all aspects of verbal art. A change in imagery is not essential to the development of poetry.[21]

He further pointed out the difference between poetic and nonpoetic images. The poetic image is defined as one of the devices of poetic language—as a device which, depending upon the problem, is as important as such other devices of poetic language as simple and negative parallelism, comparison, repetition, symmetry, hyperbole,

21. See above, p. 7. *Ed. note.*

etc., but no more important. Thus imagery becomes a part of a system of poetic devices and loses its theoretical dominance.

Shklovsky likewise repudiated the principle of artistic economy, a principle which had been strongly asserted in aesthetic theory, and opposed it with the device of "defamiliarization" and the notion of "roughened form." That is, he saw art as increasing the difficulty and span of perception "because the process of perception is an aesthetic end in itself and must be prolonged"; [22] he saw art as a means of destroying the automatism of perception; the purpose of the image is not to present the approximate meaning of its object to our understanding, but to create a special perception of the object—the creation of its "vision," and not the "recognition" of its meaning. Hence the image is usually connected with the process of defamiliarization.

The break with Potebnya was formulated definitely in Shklovsky's essay "Potebnya." [23] He repeats once more that imagery—symbolization—does not constitute the specific difference between poetic and prosaic (practical) language:

> Poetic language is distinguished from practical language by the perception of its structure. The acoustical, articulatory, or semantic aspects of poetic language may be felt. Sometimes one feels the verbal structure, the arrangement of the words, rather than their texture. The poetic image is one of the ways, but only one of the ways, of creating a perceptible structure designed to be experienced within its very own fabric. . . . The creation of a scientific poetics must begin inductively with a hypothesis built on an accumulation of evidence. That hypothesis is that poetic and prosaic languages exist, that the laws which distinguish them exist, and, finally, that these differences are to be analyzed.

These essays are to be read as the summation of the first phase of the Formalists' work. The main achievement of this period consisted in our establishment of a series of theoretical principles which provided working hypotheses for a further investigation of the data for the defeat of the current theories based on Potebnyaism. The chief strength of the Formalists, as these essays show, was neither the

22. See above, p. 12. *Ed. note.*
23. Victor Shklovsky, "Potebnya," *Poetika* (1919).

direction of their study of so-called "forms" nor the construction of a special "method"; their strength was founded securely on the fact that the specific features of the verbal arts had to be studied and that to do so it was first necessary to sort out the differing uses of poetic and practical language. Concerning form, the Formalists thought it important to change the meaning of this muddled term. It was important to destroy these traditional correlatives and so to enrich the idea of form with new significance. *The notion of "technique,"* because it has to do directly with the distinguishing features of poetic and practical speech, *is much more significant in the long-range evolution of formalism than is the notion of "form."*

4. APPLICATIONS OF THEORY:
QUESTIONS OF PLOT AND LITERARY EVOLUTION

The preliminary stage of our theoretical work had passed. We had proposed general principles bearing directly upon factual material. We now had to move closer to the material and to make the problems themselves specific. At the center stood those questions of theoretical poetics that had previously been outlined only in general form. We had to move from questions about the sound of verse to a general theory of verse. The questions about the sound of verse, when originally posed, were meant only as illustrations of the difference between poetic and practical language. We had to move from questions about "technique-in-general" to the study of the specific devices of composition, to inquiry about plot, and so on. Our interest in opposing Veselovsky's general view and, specifically, in opposing his theory of plot, developed side by side with our interest in opposing Potebnya's.

At this time, the Formalists quite naturally used literary works only as material for supporting and testing their theoretical hypotheses; we had put aside questions of convention, literary evolution, etc. Now we felt it important to widen the scope of our study, to make a preliminary survey of the data, and to allow it to establish its own kind of "laws." In this way we freed ourselves from the necessity of resorting to abstract premises and at the same time mastered the materials without losing ourselves in details.

Shklovsky, with his theory of plot and fiction, was especially important during this period. He demonstrated the presence of special devices of "plot construction" and their relation to general stylistic devices in such diverse materials as the *skaz*, Oriental tales, Cervantes' *Don Quixote*, Tolstoy's works, Sterne's *Tristram Shandy*, and so on. I do not wish to go into details—those should be treated in specialized works and not in a general essay such as this on the Formalist method—but I do wish to cover those ideas in Shklovsky's treatment of plot which have a theoretical significance beyond any relationship they might have to particular problems of plots as such. Traces of those ideas can be found in the most advanced pieces of Formalist criticism.

The first of Shklovsky's works on plot, "The Relation of Devices of Plot Construction to General Devices of Style," [24] raised a whole series of such ideas. In the first place, the proof that special devices of plot arrangement exist, a proof supported by the citation of great numbers of devices, changed the traditional notion of plot as a combination of a group of motifs and made plot a compositional rather than a thematic concept. Thus the very concept of plot was changed; *plot* was no longer synonymous with *story*. Plot construction became the natural subject of Formalist study, since plot constitutes the specific peculiarity of narrative *art*. The idea of form had been enriched, and as it lost its former abstractness, it also lost its controversial meaning. Our idea of form had begun to coincide with our idea of literature as such, with the idea of the literary fact.

Furthermore, the analogies which we established between the devices of plot construction and the devices of style had theoretical significance, for the step-by-step structure usually found in the epic was found to be analogous to sound repetition, tautology, tautological parallelism, and so on. All illustrated a general principle of verbal art based on parceling out and impeding the action.

For instance, Roland's three blows on the stone in the *Song of Roland* and the similar triple repetition common in tales may be compared, as a single type of phenomenon, with Gogol's use of synonyms and with such linguistic structures as "hoity-toity," "a

24. Victor Shklovsky, "Svyaz priyomov syuzhetoslozheniya s obschimi priyo-mami stilya," *Poetika* (1919).

diller, a dollar," etc.[25] "These variations of step-by-step construction usually do not all occur together, and attempts have been made to give each case a special explanation." Shklovsky shows how we attempt to demonstrate that the same device may reappear in diverse materials. Here we clashed with Veselovsky, who in such cases usually avoided theory and resorted to historical-genetic hypotheses. For instance, he explained epic repetition as a mechanism for the original performance (as embryonic song). But an explanation of the genetics of such a phenomenon, even if true, does not clarify the phenomenon as a fact of literature. Veselovsky and other members of the ethnographic school used to explain the peculiar motifs and plots of the *skaz* by relating literature and custom; Shklovsky did not object to making the relationship but challenged it only as an explanation of the peculiarities of the *skaz*—he challenged it as an explanation of a specifically literary fact. The study of literary genetics can clarify only the origin of a device, nothing more; poetics must explain its literary function. The genetic point of view fails to consider the device as a self-determined use of material; it does not consider how conventional materials are selected by an author, how conventional devices are transformed, or how they are made to play a structural role. The genetic point of view does not explain how a convention may disappear and its literary function remain. The literary function remains not as a simple [customary or social] experience but as a literary device retaining a significance over and beyond its connection with the convention. Character-istically, Veselovsky had contradicted himself by considering the adventures of the Greek romance as purely stylistic devices.

The Formalists naturally opposed Veselovsky's "ethnographism" because it ignored the special characteristic of the literary device and because it replaced the theoretical and evolutionary point of view with a genetic point of view.

Veselovsky saw "syncretism" as a phenomenon of primitive poetry, a result of custom, and he later was censured for this in

25. Eichenbaum gives two nonsense phrases here, *"kudy-mudy"* and *"plyushki-mlyushki."* The point is, of course, that repetition of sound alone may keep alive certain otherwise meaningless expressions. *Ed. note.*

B. Kazansky's "The Concept of Historical Poetics."[26] Kazansky repudiated the ethnographic point of view by affirming the presence of syncretic tendencies in the very nature of each art, a presence especially obvious in some periods. The Formalists naturally could not agree with Veselovsky when he touched upon general questions of literary evolution. If the clash with the Potebnyaists clarified basic principles of poetics, the clash with Veselovsky's general view and with that of his followers clarified the Formalist's views on literary evolution and, thereby, on the structure of literary history.

Shklovsky began to deal with the subject of literary evolution in the essay I cited previously, "The Relation of Devices of Plot Construction to General Devices of Style." He had encountered Veselovsky's formula, a formula broadly based on the ethnographic principle that "the purpose of new form is to express new content," and he decided to advance a completely different point of view:

> The work of art arises from a background of other works and through association with them. The form of a work of art is defined by its relation to other works of art, to forms existing prior to it. . . . Not only parody, but also any kind of work of art is created parallel to and opposed to some kind of form. *The purpose of the new form is not to express new content, but to change an old form which has lost its aesthetic quality.*

Shklovsky supported this thesis with B[roder] Christiansen's demonstration of "differentiated perceptions" or "perceptions of difference." He sees that the dynamism characteristic of art is based on this and is manifested in repeated violations of established rules. At the close of his essay, he quotes F[erdinand] Brunetière's statements that "of all the influences active in the history of literature, the chief is the influence of *work on work*," and that "one should not, without good cause, increase the number of influences upon literature, under the assumption that literature is the expression of society, nor should one confuse the history of literature with the history of morals and manners. These are entirely different things."

Shklovsky's essay marked the changeover from our study of theoretical poetics to our study of the history of literature. Our

26. B. Kazansky, "Ideya istoricheskoy poetiki," *Poetika*, I (1926), a publication of the Division of the Verbal Arts [not to be confused with the old *Poetika* of 1919, published by the *Opoyaz*].

original assumptions about form had been complicated by our observation of new features of evolutionary dynamics and their continuous variability. Our moving into the area of the history of literature was no simple expansion of our study; it resulted from the evolution of our concept of form. We found that we could not see the literary work in isolation, that we had to see its form against a background of other works rather than by itself. Thus the Formalists definitely went beyond "Formalism," if by "Formalism" one means (as some poorly informed critics usually did) some fabricated system which permitted us to be "classified," some system which zealously adapted itself to logic-chopping, or some system which joyously welcomed any dogma. Such scholastic "Formalism" was neither historical nor essentially connected with the work of the *Opoyaz*. We were not responsible for it; on the contrary, we were irreconcilably its enemies on principle.

5. PROSE FICTION:
"MOTIVATION" AND EXPOSED STRUCTURE

Later I shall return to the historical-literary work of the Formalists, but now I wish to conclude the survey of those theoretical principles and problems contained in the early work of the *Opoyaz*. The Shklovsky essay I referred to above contains still another idea which figured prominently in the subsequent study of the novel—the idea of "motivation."[27] The discovery of various techniques of plot construction (step-by-step structure, parallelism, framing, the weaving of motifs, etc.) clarified the difference between the elements used in the construction of a work and the elements comprising its material (its story, the choice of motifs, the characters, the themes, etc.). Shklovsky stressed this difference at that time because the basic problem was to show the identity of individual structural devices in the most diverse materials imaginable. The old scholarship worked exclusively with the material, taking it as the "content" and treating the remainder as an "external form" either totally without interest or of interest only to the dilettante. Hence the naive and pathetic aesthetics of our older literary critics and historians, who found "neglect of form" in Tyutchev's poetry and simply "bad form" in

27. See above, p. 30, note 9. *Ed. note.*

Nekrasov and Dostoevsky. The literary reputations of these authors were saved because their intensity of thought and mood excused their formlessness. Naturally, during the years of struggle and polemics against such a position, the Formalists directed all their forces to showing the significance of such compositional devices as motivation and ignored all other considerations. In speaking of the formal method and its evolution, we must constantly remember that many of the principles advanced by the Formalists in the years of tense struggle were significant not only as scientific principles, but also as slogans, as paradoxes sharpened for propaganda and controversy. To ignore this fact and to treat the work of the *Opoyaz* (between 1916 and 1921) in the same way as one would treat the academic scholarship is to ignore history.

The concept of motivation permitted the Formalists to approach literary works (in particular, novels and short stories) more closely and to observe the details of their structure, which Shklovsky did in two later works, *Plot Development* and *Sterne's* Tristram Shandy *and the Theory of the Novel*.[28] In these works, he studied the relationship between technique and motivation in Cervantes' *Don Quixote* and Sterne's *Tristram Shandy*. He uses *Tristram Shandy* as material for the study of the structure of the short story and the novel apart from literary history, and he studies *Don Quixote* as an instance of the transition from collections of tales (like the *Decameron*) to the novel with a single hero whose travels justify or "motivate" its episodic structure. *Don Quixote* was chosen because the devices it contains and their motivation are not fully integrated into the entire context of the novel. Material is often simply inserted, not welded in; devices of plot construction and methods of using material to further the plot structure stand out sharply, whereas later structures tend "more and more to integrate the material tightly into the very body of the novel." While analyzing "how Don Quixote was made," Shklovsky also showed the instability of the hero and concluded that

28. Victor Shklovsky, *Razvyortyvaniye syuzheta* and Tristram Shandy *Sterna i teoriya romana*, published separately in Petrograd, 1921, and later reprinted together in *O teorii prozy* (Moscow, 1925). [For the essay on *Tristram Shandy* see above, pp. 27–57.]

his "type" appeared "as the result of the business of constructing the novel." Thus the dominance of structure, of plot over material, was emphasized.

Neither a work fully "motivated" nor an art which deliberately does away with motivation and exposes the structure provides the most suitable material for the illumination of such theoretical problems. But the very existence of a work such as *Don Quixote*, with a deliberately exposed structure, confirms the relevance of these problems, confirms the fact that the problems need to be stated as problems, and confirms the fact that they are *significant* literary problems. Moreover, we were able to explain works of literature entirely in the light of these theoretical problems and principles, as Shklovsky did with *Tristram Shandy*. Shklovsky not only used the book to illustrate our theoretical position, he gave it new significance and once more attracted attention to it. Studied against the background of an interest in the *structure* of the novel, Sterne became a contemporary; people spoke about him, people who previously had found in his novel only boring chatter or eccentricities, or who had prejudged it from the point of view of its notorious "sentimentalism," a characteristic for which Sterne is as little to blame as Gogol for "realism."

Shklovsky pointed out Sterne's deliberate laying bare of his methods of constructing *Tristram Shandy* and asserted that Sterne had "exaggerated" the structure of the novel. He had shown his awareness of form by his manner of violating it and by his manner of assembling the novel's contents. In his conclusion to the essay, Shklovsky formulated the difference between plot and story:

> The idea of plot is too often confused with the description of events— with what I propose provisionally to call the *story*. The story is, in fact, only material for plot formulation. The plot of *Evgeny Onegin* is, there-fore, not the romance of the hero with Tatyana, but the fashioning of the subject of this story as produced by the introduction of interrupting digressions. . . .
>
> The forms of art are explainable by the laws of art; they are not justified by their realism. Slowing the action of a novel is not accom-plished by introducing rivals, for example, but by simply *transposing*

parts. In so doing the artist makes us aware of the aesthetic laws which underlie both the transposition and the slowing down of the action.[29]

My essay "How Gogol's 'Greatcoat' Was Made,"[30] also considers the structure of the novel, comparing the problem of plot with the problem of the *skaz*—the problem of structure based upon the narrator's manner of telling what had happened. I tried to show that Gogol's text "was made up of living speech patterns and vocalized emotions," that words and sentences are selected and joined by Gogol as they are in the oral *skaz*, in which articulation, mimicry, sound gestures, and so on, play a special role. From this point of view I showed how the structure of "The Greatcoat" imparts a grotesque tone to the tale by replacing the usual humor of the *skaz* (with its anecdotes, puns, etc.) with sentimental-melodramatic declamation. I discussed, in this connection, the end of "The Greatcoat" as the apotheosis of the grotesque—not unlike the mute scene in *The Inspector General*.[31] The traditional line of argument about Gogol's "romanticism" and "realism" proved unnecessary and unilluminating.

Thus we began to make some progress with the problem of the study of prose. The line between the idea of plot as structure and the idea of the story as material was drawn; this explanation of the typical techniques of plot construction opened the door for work on the history and theory of the novel; and furthermore, the *skaz* was treated as the structural basis of the plotless short story. These works have influenced a whole series of recent studies by persons not directly connected with the *Opoyaz*.

6. POETRY: METER VERSUS A COMPLETE LINGUISTIC PROSODY: SYNTAX, INTONATION, PHONEMICS

As our theoretical work broadened and deepened it naturally became specialized—the more so because persons who were only beginning their work or who had been working independently joined the *Opoyaz* group. Some of them specialized in the problems

29. See above, p. 57. *Ed. note.*

30. Boris Eichenbaum, "Kak sledana 'Shinel' Gogolya," *Poetika* (1919).

31. The final scene, in which not a word is spoken for a minute and a half as the curtain slowly falls. *Ed. note.*

of poetry, others in the problems of prose. The Formalists insisted upon keeping clear the demarcation between poetry and prose in order to counterbalance the Symbolists, who were then attempting to erase the boundary line both in theory and in practice by painstakingly attempting to discover meter in prose.[32]

The earlier sections of this essay show the intensity of our work on prose. We were pioneers in the area. Several Western works resembled ours (in particular, such observations on story material as Wilhelm Dibelius' *Englische Romankunst*, 1910), but they had little relevance to our theoretical problems and principles. In our work on prose we felt almost free from tradition, but in dealing with verse the situation was different. The great number of works by Western and Russian literary theorists, the numerous practical and theoretical experiments of the Symbolists, and the special literature of the controversies over the concepts of rhythm and meter (produced between 1910 and 1917) complicated our study of poetry. The Futurists, in that same period, were creating new verse forms, and this complicated things still more. Given such conditions, it was difficult for us to pose the right problems. Many persons, instead of returning to basic questions, were concerned with special problems of metrics or with trying to put the accumulation of systems and opinions in good order. Meanwhile, we had no general theory of poetry: no theoretical elucidations of verse rhythm, of the connection of rhythm and syntax, of the sounds of verse (the Formalists had indicated only a few linguistic premises), of poetic diction and semantics, and so on. In other words, the nature of verse as such remained essentially obscure. We had to draw away from particular problems of metrics and to approach verse from some more disciplined perspective. We had, first of all, to pose the problem of rhythm so that it did not rest on metrics and would include a more substantial part of poetic speech.[33]

Here, as in the previous section, I shall dwell upon the problem

32. See especially Andrey Bely's *Simvolizm* (Moscow, 1910). *Ed. note.*

33. One might compare this aspect of the Formalists' work with the recent attempts of the structural linguists to incorporate such rhythmic and acoustical elements as stress, pitch, juncture, etc., into their study of the total linguistic pattern. *Ed. note.*

of verse only insofar as its exploration led to a new theoretical view
of verbal art or a new view of the nature of poetic speech. Our
position was stated first in Osip Brik's "On Rhythmic-Syntactic
Figures" [1920], an unpublished lecture delivered before the *Opoyaz*
group and, apparently, not even written out [Brik's lecture was
published in 1927 in *New Left*]. Brik demonstrated that verse
contained stable syntactical figures indissolubly connected with
rhythm. Thus rhythm was no longer thought of as an abstraction;
it was made relevant to the very linguistic fabric of verse—the
phrase. Metrics became a kind of background, significant, like the
alphabet, for the reading and writing of verse. Brik's step was as
important for the study of verse as the discovery of the relation of
plot to structure was for the study of prose. The discovery that
rhythmic patterns are related to the grammatical patterns of
sentences destroyed the notion that rhythm is a superficial
appendage, something floating on the surface of speech. Our theory
of verse was founded on the analysis of rhythm as the structural basis
of verse, a basis which of itself determined all of its parts—both
acoustical and nonacoustical. A superior theory of verse, which
would make metrics but a kindergarten preparation, was in sight.
The Symbolists and the group led by Bely, despite their attempts,
could not travel our road because they still saw the central problem
as metrics in isolation.

But Brik's work merely hinted at the possibility of a new way;
like his first essay, "Sound Repetitions," [34] it was limited to showing
examples and arranging them into groups. From Brik's lecture one
could move either into new problems or into the simple classification
and cataloging, or systematizing, of the material. The lecture was
not necessarily an expression of the formal method. V[ictor]
Zhirmunsky continued the work of classification in *The Composition
of Lyric Verse*.[35] Zhirmunsky, who did not share the theoretical
principles of the *Opoyaz*, was interested in the formal method as only
one of the possible scientific approaches to the division of materials
into various groups and headings. Given his understanding of the
formal method, he could do nothing else; he accepted any super-

34. Osip Brik, "Zvukovye povtory," [*Poetika* (1919)].
35. Victor Zhirmunsky, *Kompozitsiya liricheskikh stikhotvoreny* (Petrograd, 1921).

ficial feature as a basis for the grouping of materials. Hence the unvarying cataloging and the pedantic tone of all of Zhirmunsky's theoretical work. Such works were not a major influence in the general evolution of the formal method; in themselves they merely emphasized the tendency (evidently historically inevitable) to give the formal method an academic quality. It is not surprising, therefore, that Zhirmunsky later completely withdrew from the *Opoyaz* over a difference of opinion about the principles he stated repeatedly in his last works (especially in his introduction to the translation of O[skar] Walzel's *The Problem of Form in Prose* [1923]).

My book, *Verse Melody*,[36] which was prepared as a study of the phonetics of verse and so was related to a whole group of Western works (by Sievers, Saran, etc.), was relevant to Brik's work on rhythmic-syntactic figures. I maintained that stylistic differences were usually chiefly lexical:

> With that we drop the idea of versification as such, and take up poetic language in general. . . . We have to find something related to the *poetic phrase* that does not also lead us away from the *poetry* itself, something bordering on both phonetics and semantics. This "something" is syntax.

I did not examine the rhythmic-syntactic phenomena in isolation, but as part of an examination of the structural significance of metrical and vocal intonation. I felt it especially important both to assert the idea of a *dominant*, upon which a given poetic style is organized, and to isolate the idea of "melody" as a system of intonations from the idea of the general "musicality" of verse. On this basis, I proposed to distinguish three fundamental styles of lyric poetry: declamatory (oratorical), melodic, and conversational. My entire book is devoted to the peculiarities of the melodic style—to peculiarities in the material of the lyrics of Zhukovsky, Tyutchev, Lermontov, and Fet. Avoiding ready-made schematizations, I ended the book with the conviction that "in scientific work, I consider the ability to see facts far more important than the construction of a system. Theories are necessary to clarify facts; in reality, theories are made of facts. Theories perish and change, but the facts they help discover and support remain."

36. Boris Eichenbaum, *Melodika russkovo liricheskovo stikha* (Petrograd, 1922).

The tradition of specialized metrical studies still continued among the Symbolist theoreticians (Bely, Bryusov, Bobrov, Chudovsky, and others), but it gradually turned into precise statistical enumeration and lost what had been its dominant characteristic. Here the metrical studies of Boris Tomashevsky, concluded in his text *Russian Versification*,[37] played the most significant role. Thus, as the study of metrics became secondary, a subsidiary discipline with a very limited range of problems, the general theory of verse entered its first stage.

Tomashevsky's "Pushkin's Iambic Pentameter"[38] outlined the entire previous course of developments within the formal method, including its attempt to broaden and enrich the notion of poetic rhythm and to relate it to the structure of poetic language. The essay also attempted to go beyond the idea of meter in language. Hence the basic charge against Bely and his school: "The problem of rhythm is not conformity to imaginary meters; it is rather the distribution of expiratory energy within a single wave—the line itself." In "The Problems of Poetic Rhythm"[39] Tomashevsky expressed this with perfect clarity of principle. Here the earlier conflict between meter and rhythm is resolved by applying the idea of rhythm in verse to all of the elements of speech that play a part in the structure of verse. The rhythms of phrasal intonation and euphony (alliterations, etc.) are placed side by side with the rhythm of word accent. Thus we came to see the line as *a special form of speech* which functions as a single unit in the creation of poetry. We no longer saw the line as something which could create a "rhythmic variation" by resisting or adjusting to the metrical form (a view which Zhirmunsky continued to defend in his new work, *Introduction to Metrics*[40]). Tomashevsky wrote that:

> Poetic speech is *organized* in terms of its sounds. Taken singly, any phonetic element is subject to rules and regulations, but sound is a *complex* phenomenon. Thus classical metrics singles out accent and normalizes it by its rules. . . . But it takes little effort to shake the

37. Boris Tomashevsky, *Russkoye stikhoslozheniye: Metrika* (Petrograd, 1923).

38. Boris Tomashevsky, "Pyatistopny iamb Pushkina," *Ocherki po poetike Pushkina* [*Essays on the Poetics of Pushkin*] (Berlin, 1923).

39. Boris Tomashevsky, "Problema stikhotvornovo ritma," *Literaturnaya mysl* [*Literary Thought*], II (1922).

40. Boris Tomashevsky, *Vvedeniye v metriku: Teoriya stikha* [*Introduction to Metrics: The Theory of Verse*] (Leningrad, 1925).

authority of traditional forms, because the notion persisted that the nature of verse is not fully explained by a single distinguishing feature, that poetry exists in "secondary" features, that a recognizable rhythm exists alongside meter, that poetry can be created by imposing a pattern on only these secondary features, and *that speech without meter may sound like poetry.*

The important idea of a "rhythmic impulse" (which had figured earlier in Brik's work) with a general rhythmic function is maintained here:

Rhythmic devices may participate in various degrees in the creation of an artistic-rhythmic effect; this or that device may dominate various works—this or that means may be the *dominant.* The use of a given rhythmic device determines the character of the particular rhythm of the work. On this basis poetry may be classified as accented-metrical poetry (e.g., the description of the Battle of Poltava [41]), intoned-melodic poetry (the verses of Zhukovsky), or harmonic poetry (common during the recent years of Russian Symbolism).

Poetic form, so understood, is not contrasted with anything outside itself—with a "content" which has been laboriously set inside this "form"—but is understood as the genuine content of poetic speech. Thus the very idea of form, as it had been understood in earlier works, emerged with a new and more adequate meaning.

7. TOWARD A MORE COMPLETE PROSODY

In his essay "On Czech Versification" Roman Jakobson pointed out new problems in the general theory of poetic rhythm.[42] He opposed the [earlier] theory that "verse adapts itself completely to the spirit of the language," that is, that "form does not resist the material [it shapes]" with the theory that "poetic form is the organized coercion of language." [43] He applied this refinement of

41. Pushkin, *Poltava. Ed. note.*

42. Roman Jakobson, *O cheshskom stikhe preimuschestvenno v sopostavlenii s russkim* (Berlin, 1923).

43. Jakobson is close here to John Crowe Ransom's theory of determinate and indeterminate factors, in which Ransom argues that the intended meaning of a poem is roughened, sometimes deliberately, as the poet attempts to give it a form; and that the form is likewise roughened as the poet attempts to put his meaning into it. *The New Criticism* (Norfolk, Conn.: New Directions, 1941), pp. 316–317. *Ed. note.*

the more orthodox view—a refinement in keeping with the formalist method—to the question of the difference between the phonetic qualities of practical language and those of poetic language. Although Jakubinsky had [for example] noted that the dissimilation of liquid consonants [*l* and *r*] is relatively infrequent in poetry, Jakobson showed that it existed in both poetic and practical language but that in practical language it is "accidental"; in poetic language it is, "so to speak, contrived; these are two distinct phenomena." [44]

In the same essay Jakobson also clarified the principle distinction between emotional and poetic language (a distinction he had previously considered in his first book, *Modern Russian Poetry*):

> Although poetry may use the methods of emotive language, it uses them only for *its own* purposes. The similiarities between the two kinds of language and the use of poetic language in the way that emotive language is used frequently leads to the assumption that the two are identical. The assumption is mistaken because it fails to consider the radical difference of *function* between the two kinds of language.

In this connection Jakobson refuted the attempts of [Maurice] Grammont [45] and other prosodists to explain the phonetic structure of poetry in terms either of onomatopoeia or of the emotional connection between sounds and images. "Phonetic structure," he wrote, "is not always a structure of audible images, nor is a structure of audible images always a method of emotional language." Jakobson's book was typical because it constantly went beyond the limits of its particular, special theme (the prosody of Czech verse) and shed light on general questions about the theory of poetic language and verse. Thus his book ends with a whole essay on Mayakovsky [a Russian poet], an essay complemented by his earlier piece on Khlebnikov [another Russian poet].

In my own work on Anna Akhmatova [46] I also attempted to raise basic theoretical questions about the theory of verse—questions of

44. Jakubinsky had already pointed out the excessive complexity of the idea of "practical speech" and the impossibility of analyzing it in terms of function (conversational, oratorical, scientific, and so on); see his essay, "O dialogicheskoy rechi," ["On Dialogic Speech"], *Russkaya rech* [*Russian Speech*], I (1923).

45. Maurice Grammont, *Le vers français, ses moyens d'expression, son harmonie* (Paris, 1913). *Ed. note.*

46. Boris Eichenbaum, *Anna Akhmatova* ([Petrograd], 1923).

the relation of rhythm to syntax and intonation, the relation of the sound of verse to its articulation, and lastly, the relation of poetic diction to semantics. Referring to a book which Yury Tynyanov was then preparing, I pointed out that "as words get into verse they are, as it were, taken out of ordinary speech. They are surrounded by a new aura of meaning and perceived not against the background of speech in general but against the background of poetic speech." I also indicated that the formation of collateral meanings, which disrupts ordinary verbal associations, is the chief peculiarity of the semantics of poetry.[47]

Until then, the original connection between the formal method and linguistics had been growing considerably weaker. The difference that had developed between our problems was so great that we no longer needed the special support of the linguists, especially the support of those who were psychologically oriented. In fact, some of the work of the linguists was objectionable in principle. Tynyanov's *The Problem of Poetic Language*,[48] which had appeared just then, emphasized the difference between the study of psychological linguistics and the study of poetic language and style. This book showed the intimate relation that exists between the meanings of words and the poetic structure itself; it added new meaning to the idea of poetic rhythm and initiated the Formalists' investigation not only of acoustics and syntax, but also of the shades of meaning peculiar to poetic speech. In the introduction Tynyanov says:

> The study of poetry has of late been quite rewarding. Undoubtedly the prospect in the near future is for development in the whole field, although we all remember the systematic beginning of the study. But the study of poetry has been kept isolated from questions of poetic language *and* style; the study of the latter is kept isolated from the study of the former. The impression is given that neither the poetic language itself nor the poetic style itself has any connection with poetry, that the one does not depend upon the other. The idea of "poetic language," which was advanced not so long ago and is now changing, undoubtedly invited a certain looseness by its breadth and by the vagueness of its content, a content based on psychological linguistics.

47. This is the nearest the Formalists came to pursuing the line taken by the New Critics—the discussion of poetry as compacted meaning. *Ed. note.*
48. Yury Tynyanov, *Problema stikhotvornovo yazyka* (Leningrad, 1924).

Among the general questions of poetics revived and illuminated by this book, that of the idea of the "material" is most fundamental. The generally accepted view saw an opposition between form and content; when the distinction was made purely verbal, it lost its meaning. In fact, as I have already mentioned, our view gave form the significance of a thing complete in itself and strengthened it by considering the work of art in relation to its purpose. Our concept of form required no complement—except that other, artistically insignificant, kind of form.[49] Tynyanov showed that the materials of verbal art were neither all alike nor all equally important, that "one feature may be prominent at the expense of the rest, so that the remainder is deformed and sometimes degraded to the level of a neutral prop." Hence the conclusion that "the idea of 'material' does not lie beyond the limits of form; the material itself is a formal element. To confuse it with external structural features is a mistake." After this, Tynyanov could make the notion of form more complex by showing that form is dynamic:

> The unity of the work is not a closed, symmetrical whole, but an unfolding, dynamic whole. Its elements are not static indications of equality and complexity, but always dynamic indications of correlation and integration. The form of literary works must be thought of as dynamic.

Rhythm is here presented as the fundamental specific factor which permeates all the elements of poetry. The objective sign of

49. See Cleanth Brooks' "articles of faith," which include the convictions that "*in a successful work, form and content cannot be separated,*" and that "*form is meaning.*" "The Formalist Critics," *Kenyon Review,* XIII (1951), p. 72. Both the Russian Formalists and Brooks go beyond the old form-content dichotomy which sees content either as "meaning" or as "material" and form as a kind of superficial glamorization of the content, a sugar coating to make the content palatable. The problems raised by the old view are formidable and pervasive. To give just one example, is the alliteration in "Poor soul, the center of my sinful earth" an element of form, or an element of content? It "glamorizes" the line, yet it also links the central concepts. If we change the alliteration pattern, and hence the form, by making "sinful" read "evil," we seem to imply that the "poor soul" is surrounded by a wicked earth, rather than that it is infested with the earth's wickedness. In brief, to alter the form is to change the content. *Ed. note.*

poetic rhythm is the establishment of a *rhythmic group* whose *unity* and *richness* exist side by side with each other. And again, Tynyanov affirms the principal distinction between prose and poetry:

> Poetry, as opposed to prose, tends toward unity and richness ranged around an uncommon object. This very "uncommonness" prevents the main point of the poem from being smoothed over. Indeed, it asserts the object with a new force. . . . Any element of prose brought into the poetic pattern is transformed into verse by that feature of it which asserts its function and which thus has two aspects: the emphasis of the structure—the versification—and the deformation of the uncommon object.

Tynyanov also raises the question of semantics: "In verse are not the ordinary semantic meanings of the words so distorted (a fact which makes complete paraphrase impossible) that the usual principles governing their arrangement no longer apply?" The entire second part of Tynyanov's book answers this question by defining the precise relation between rhythm and semantics. The facts show clearly that oral presentations are unified in part by rhythm. "This is shown in a more forceful and more compact integration of connectives than occurs in ordinary speech; words are made correlative by their positions"; prose lacks this feature.

Thus the Formalists abandoned Potebnya's theory and accepted the conclusions connected with it on a new basis, and a new perspective opened on to the theory of verse. Tynyanov's work permitted us to grasp even the remotest implications of these new problems. It became clear even to those only casually acquainted with the *Opoyaz* that the essence of our work consisted not in some kind of static "formal method," but in a study of the specific peculiarities of verbal art—we were not advocates of a method, but students of an object. Again, Tynyanov stated this:

> The object of a study claiming to be a study of art ought to be so specific that it is distinguished from other areas of intellectual activity and uses them for its own materials and tools. Each work of art represents a complex interaction of many factors; consequently, the job of the student is the definition of the specific character of this interaction.

8. STYLE, GENRE, AND HISTORICAL CRITICISM

Earlier I noted that the problem of the diffusion and change of form—the problem of literary evolution—is raised naturally along with theoretical problems. The problem of literary evolution arises in connection with a reconsideration of Veselovsky's view of *skaz* motifs and devices; the answer ("new form is not to express new content, but to replace old form") led to a new understanding of form. If form is understood as the very content, constantly changing according to its dependence upon previous "images," then we naturally had to approach it without abstract, ready-made, unalterable, classical schemes; and we had to consider specifically its historical sense and significance. The approach developed its own kind of dual perspective: the perspective of theoretical study (like Shklovsky's "Development of Plot" and my "Vērse Melody"), which centered on a given theoretical problem and its applicability to the most diverse materials, and the perspective of historical studies—studies of literary evolution as such. The combination of these two perspectives, both organic to the subsequent development of the formal school, raised a series of new and very complex problems, many of which are still unsolved and even undefined.

Actually, the original attempt of the Formalists to take a particular structural device and to establish its identity in diverse materials became an attempt to differentiate, to understand, the *function* of a device in each given case. This notion of functional significance was gradually pushed toward the foreground and the original idea of the device pushed into the background. This kind of sorting out of its own general ideas and principles has been characteristic of our work throughout the evolution of the formal method. We have no dogmatic position to bind us and shut us off from facts. We do not answer for our schematizations; they may require change, refinement, or correction when we try to apply them to previously unknown facts. Work on specific materials compelled us to speak of functions and thus to revise our idea of the device. The theory itself demanded that we turn to history.

Here again we were confronted with the traditional academic sciences and the preferences of critics. In our student days the academic history of literature was limited chiefly to biographical and psychological studies of various writers—only the "greats," of course. Critics no longer made attempts to construct a history of Russian literature as a whole, attempts which evidenced the intention of bringing the great historical materials into a system; nevertheless, the traditions established by earlier histories (like A. N. Pypin's *History of Russian Literature*) retained their scholarly authority, the more so because the following generation had decided not to pursue such broad themes. Meanwhile, the chief role was played by such general and somewhat vague notions as "realism" and "romanticism" (realism was said to be better than romanticism); evolution was understood as gradual perfection, as progress (from romanticism to realism); succession [of literary schools] as the peaceful transfer of the inheritance from father to son. But generally, there was no notion of literature as such; material taken from the history of social movements, from biography, etc. had replaced it entirely.

This primitive historicism, which led away from literature, naturally provoked the Symbolist theoreticians and critics into a denial of any kind of historicism. Their own discussions of literature, consequently, developed into impressionistic "etudes" and "silhouettes," and they indulged in a widespread "modernization" of old writers, transforming them into "eternal companions." The history of literature was silently (and sometimes aloud) declared unnecessary.

We had to demolish the academic tradition and to eliminate the bias of the journalists [the Symbolist theoreticians]. We had to advance against the first a new understanding of literary evolution and of literature itself—without the idea of progress and peaceful succession, without the ideas of realism and romanticism, without materials foreign to literature—as a specific order of phenomena, a specific order of material. We had to act against the second by pointing out concrete historical facts, fluctuating and changing forms, by pointing to the necessity of taking into account the specific functions of this or that device—in a word, we had to draw the line between the literary work as a definite historical fact and a free interpretation of it from the standpoint of contemporary literary needs, tastes, or interests. Thus the basic passion for our historical-literary work had to be a passion for destruction and negation, and such was the original tone of our theoretical attacks; our work later assumed a calmer note when we went on to solutions of particular problems.

That is why the first of our historical-literary pronouncements came in the form of theses expressed almost against our will in connection with some specific material. A particular question would unexpectedly lead to the formulation of a general problem, a problem that inextricably mixed theoretical and historical considerations. In this sense Tynyanov's *Dostoevsky and Gogol*[50] and Shklovsky's *Rozanov*[51] were typical.

Tynyanov's basic problem was to show that Dostoevsky's *The Village of Stepanchikovo* is a parody, that behind its first level is hidden a second—it is a parody of Gogol's *Correspondence with Friends*. But his treatment of this particular question was overshadowed by a whole theory of parody [which he developed to solve the particular problem], a theory of parody as a stylistic device (stylized parody) and as one of the manifestations (having great historical-literary significance) of the dialectical development of literary groups. With this arose the problem of "succession" and "tradition" and, hence, the basic problems of literary evolution were posed [as part of the study of style]:

> When one speaks of "literary tradition" or "succession" . . . usually one implies a certain kind of direct line uniting the younger and older representatives of a known literary branch. Yet the matter is much more complicated. There is no continuing direct line; there is rather a departure, a pushing away from the known point—a struggle. . . . Any literary succession is first of all a struggle, a destruction of old values and a reconstruction of old elements.

"Literary evolution" was complicated by the notion of struggle, of periodic uprisings, and so lost its old suggestion of peaceful and gradual development. Against this background, the literary relationship between Dostoevsky and Gogol was shown to be that of a complicated struggle.

50. Yury Tynyanov, *Dostoevsky i Gogol* (Petrograd, 1921).
51. Victor Shklovsky, *Rozanov* (Petrograd, 1921).

In his *Rozanov*, Shklovsky showed, almost in the absence of basic themes, a whole theory of literary evolution which even then reflected the current discussion of such problems in *Opoyaz*. Shklovsky showed that literature moves forward in a broken line:

> In each literary epoch there is not one literary school, but several. They exist simultaneously, with one of them representing the high point of the current orthodoxy. The others exist uncanonized, mutely; in Pushkin's time, for example, the courtly tradition of [Wilhelm] Kuchelbecker and [Alexander] Greboyedov existed simultaneously with the tradition of Russian vaudeville verse and with such other traditions as that of the pure adventure novel of Bulgarin.

The moment the old art is canonized, new forms are created on a lower level. A "young line" is created which

> grows up to replace the old, as the vaudevillist Belopyatkin is transformed into a Nekrasov (see Brik's discussion of the relationship); a direct descendent of the eighteenth century, Tolstoy, creates a new novel (see the work of Boris Eichenbaum); Blok makes the themes and times of the gypsy ballad acceptable, and Chekhov introduces the "alarm clock" into Russian literature. Dostoevsky introduced the devices of the dime novel into the mainstream of literature. Each new literary school heralds a revolution, something like the appearance of a new class. But, of course, this is only an analogy. The vanquished line is not obliterated, it does not cease to exist. It is only knocked from the crest; it lies dormant and may again arise as a perennial pretender to the throne. Moreover, in reality the matter is complicated by the fact that the new hegemony is usually not a pure revival of previous forms but is made more complex by the presence of features of the younger schools and with features, now secondary, inherited from its predecessors on the throne.

Shklovsky is discussing the dynamism of genres, and he interprets Rozanov's books as embodiments of a new genre, as a new type of novel in which the parts are unconnected by motivation. "Thematically, Rozanov's books are characterized by the elevation of new themes; compositionally, by the revealed device." As part of this general theory, we introduced the notion of the "dialectical self-creation of new forms," that is, hidden in the new form we saw both analogies with other kinds of cultural development and proof of the independence of the phenomena of literary evolution.[52] In a simplified form, this theory quickly changed hands and, as always happens, became a simple and fixed scheme—very handy for critics. Actually, we have here only a general outline of evolution surrounded by a whole series of complicated conditions. From this general outline the Formalists moved on to a more consistent solution of historical-literary problems and facts, specifying and refining their original theoretical premises.

9. LITERARY HISTORY AND LITERARY EVOLUTION

Given our understanding of literary evolution as the dialectical change of forms, we did not go back to the study of those materials which had held the central position in the old-fashioned historical-literary work. We studied literary evolution insofar as it bore a distinctive character and only to the extent that it stood alone, quite independent of other aspects of culture. In other words, we stuck exclusively to facts in order not to pass into an endless number of indefinite "connections" and "correspondences" which would do nothing at all to explain literary evolution. We did not take up questions of the biography and psychology of the artist because we assumed that these questions, in themselves serious and complex, must take their places in other sciences. We felt it important to find indications of historical regularity in evolution—that is why we ignored all that seemed, from this point of view, "circumstantial," not concerned with [literary] history. We were interested in the very process of evolution, in the very *dynamics* of literary form, insofar as it was possible to observe them in the facts of the past. For us, the central problem of the history of literature is the problem of evolution without personality—the study of literature as a *self-formed social phenomenon*. As a result, we found extremely significant both the question of the formation and changes of genres and the question of how "second-rate" and "popular" literature contributed to the formation of genres. Here we had only to distinguish that popular literature which prepared the way for the formation of new genres from that which arose out of their decay and which offered material for the study of historical inertia.

52. See above, pp. 92–95. *Ed. note.*

On the other hand, we were not interested in the past, in isolated historical facts, as such; we did not busy ourselves with the "restoration" of this or that epoch because we happened to like it. History gave us what the present could not—a stable body of material. But, precisely for this reason, we approached it with a stock of theoretical problems and principles suggested in part by the facts of contemporary literature. The Formalists, then, characteristically had a close interest in contemporary literature and also reconciled criticism and scholarship. The earlier literary historians had, to a great extent, kept themselves aloof from contemporary literature; the Symbolists had subordinated scholarship to criticism. We saw in the history of literature not so much a special theoretical *subject* as a special *approach*, a special cross section of literature. The character of our historical-literary work involved our being drawn not only to historical conclusions, but also to theoretical conclusions—to the posing of new theoretical problems and to the testing of old.

From 1922 to 1924 a whole series of Formalist studies of literary history was written, many of which, because of contemporary market conditions, remain unpublished and are known only as reports. * * *[53] There is, of course, not space enough here to speak of such works in detail. They usually took up "secondary" writers (those who form the background of literature) and carefully explained the traditions of their work, noting changes in genres, styles, and so on. As a result, many forgotten names and facts came to light, current estimates were shown to be inaccurate, traditional ideas changed, and, chiefly, the very process of literary evolution became clearer. The working out of this material has only begun. A new series of problems is before us: further differentiation of

53. The deleted material contains a listing of some Formalist works, including: Yury Tynanyov's "Verse Forms of Nekrasov," "The Question of Tyutchev," "Tyutchev and Pushkin," "Tyutchev and Heine," "The Ode as a Declamatory Genre"; Boris Tomashevsky's "Gavriliada," "Pushkin, a Reader of French Poets," "Pushkin," "Pushkin and Boileau," "Pushkin and La Fontaine"; Boris Eichenbaum's *Lermontov*, "Problems of the Poetics of Pushkin," "Pushkin's Path to Prose," "Nekrasov"; Victor Vinogradov's "Plot and Structure of Gogol's 'The Nose,'" "Plot and Architectonics of Dostoevsky's Novel *Poor People*," "Gogol and the Realistic School," "Studies on the Style of Gogol"; and Victor Zhirmunsky's "Byron and Pushkin."

theoretical and historical literary ideas, introduction of new material, posing new questions, and so on.

10. SUMMARY

I shall conclude with a general summary. The evolution of the formal method, which I have tried to present, has the look of a sequential development of theoretical principles—apart from the individual roles each of us played. Actually, the work of the *Opoyaz* group was genuinely collective. It was this way, obviously, because from the very beginning we understood the historical nature of our task; we did not see it as the personal affair of this or that individual. This was our chief connection with the times. Science itself is still evolving, and we are evolving with it. I shall indicate briefly the evolution of the formal method during these ten years:

1. From the original outline of the conflict of poetic language with practical we proceeded to differentiate the idea of practical language by its various functions (Jakubinsky) and to delimit the methods of poetic and emotional languages (Jakobson). Along with this we became interested in studying oratorical speech because it was close to practical speech but distinguished from it by function, and we spoke about the necessity of a revival of the poetic of rhetoric.[54]

2. From the general idea of form, in its new sense, we proceeded to the idea of technique, and from here, to the idea of function.

3. From the idea of poetic rhythm as opposed to meter we proceeded to the idea of rhythm as a constructive element in the total poem and thus to an understanding of verse as a special form of speech having special linguistic (syntactical, lexical, and semantic) features.

4. From the idea of plot as structure we proceeded to an understanding of material in terms of its motivation, and from here to an understanding of material as an element participating in the construction but subordinate to the character of the dominant formal idea.

5. From the ascertainment of a single device applicable to various materials we proceeded to differentiate techniques according to

54. *Lef* [*Left*], I, No. 5 (1925).

function and from here to the question of the evolution of form—
that is, to the problem of historical-literary study.

A whole new series of problems faces us, as Tynyanov's latest
essay, "Literary Fact," shows.[55] Here the question of the relation
between life and literature is posed, a question which many persons
"answer" on the basis of a simple-minded dilettantism. Examples of
how life becomes literature are shown and, conversely, of how
literature passes into life:

> During the period of its deterioration a given genre is shoved from the
> center toward the periphery, but in its place, from the trivia of literature,
> from literature's backyard, and from life itself, new phenomena flow
> into the center.

Although I deliberately called this essay "The Theory of the
'Formal Method,'" I gave, obviously, a sketch of its evolution.
We have no theory that can be laid out as a fixed, ready-made
system. For us theory and history merge not only in words, but in
fact. We are too well trained by history itself to think that it can be
avoided. When we feel that we have a theory that explains everything, a ready-made theory explaining all past and future events
and therefore needing neither evolution nor anything like it—then
we must recognize that the formal method has come to an end, that
the spirit of scientific investigation has departed from it. As yet, that
has not happened.

Boris Eichenbaum, "Teoriya 'formalnovo metoda,'" *Literatura: Teoriya,
kritika, polemika* [*Literature: Theory, Criticism, Polemics*] (Leningrad, 1927).

55. *Lef*, II, No. 6 (1925).

Index

Symbolism, xii–xiv, 4, 7, 8, 82, 93, 105–106, 108–109, 112–115, 123–124, 126, 133

Syntax, 122–127

"Tale of Balda," 69

Techniques, imperceptible, 93; perceptible, 93

Tension, 72

"Thematics," xii, 25, 93

Theme, 61, 62–66, 67, 93

"Theory of the 'Formal Method,' The," xv

Time, 66, 77; displacement, 28–30, 52, 54, 74; story, 36–37, 77–78; reading, 77–78

Tolstoy, Alexey, 65, 83

Tolstoy, Leo, xv, 3, 12, 13–18, 21, 22, 34, 43, 84, 85–86, 99, 116

Tomashevsky, Boris, xii, 25, 26, 126–127

Tristram Shandy, 25–57, 116, 120–121

Trotsky, Leo, 99–100

Turgenev, Ivan S., 12, 30, 64, 74

Tynyanov, Yury, 129–134

Tyutchev, Fyodor, 6, 119, 125, 129, 131

Veselovsky, Alexander, xi, xii, 10, 105, 107, 115, 117–118, 121

War and Peace, 3, 15–17, 22, 84–85

Warren, Austin, ix, xiv

Wellek, René, ix, xiv, xv

Zeitlin, Alexander, 100

Zhirmunsky, Victor, xvi, 124–126

Zhukovsky, Vasily A., 125